Looking at Teaching Through the Lens of the FFT Clusters

Study Guide
Set 4

The Danielson Group
contact@danielsongroup.org

Contents

Study Guide Overview

Introduction

Welcome to the FFT (Framework for Teaching) series of Clusters Study Guides. Their purpose is to guide professioncommunities as they engage in activities and discussions to enhance their own practices and the practices of their colleagues. An Instructional Set of lesson artifacts (that may include lesson plans, a video of the entire lesson, student work, and teacher commentary) is used as a resource for each Study Guide. The combination of the Study Guide activities, the Instructional Set artifacts, and the user's experience yields a powerful method of examining teaching and applying learning to one's own practice.

Background

The Instructional Sets are actual lessons led by teachers with their own students. The videos run the duration of the lesson. The teachers and students are not actors, and the lessons are part of their curriculum, not something that was scripted for the Study Guides. The Danielson Group is extremely appreciative of the teachers and their students for providing an opportunity for others to view authentic classroom artifacts for the purpose of professional growth.

A team of educational practitioners and Danielson Group consultants, who have extensive experience in effective teaching practices and professional development training, created this Study Guide series (see Appendix A for the team members). The team received rigorous training on the FFT

Clusters and on how to analyze the teaching and learning evident in the Instructional Sets. They worked with Charlotte Danielson, lead consultants, and each other to create the contents of the Guides.

The series includes many Study Guides. Each Guide was written for a group of accompanying Instructional Sets. The collection includes a sampling of K–12 lessons in Mathematics, English Language Arts, Science, Social Studies, and Science Technology. The majority of lessons are in Mathematics and English Language Arts. Analyzing lessons from a variety of grades and subject areas provides opportunities for educators to stretch their analytic skills and enhance their understanding of the FFT Clusters. A list of the Instructional Sets can be found in Appendix B.

The team created a Record of Evidence for each Instructional Set. The activities portion of the Study Guide provides highlights of the Instructional Set, whereas the Record provides an extensive list of evidence gleaned from the video and artifacts for the FFT Clusters. A Record also includes interpretations of the evidence by the authors who were trained as coders. For each Record, two coders analyzed an Instructional Set independently, then compared their records to produce a composite version for the Study Guide. The Record of Evidence does not contain scores or evaluations, since the evidence is intended for use in professional conversations.

Contents of the Study Guides

Each Study Guide provides a multi-step process for examining the contents of an Instructional Set, reflecting on and discussing its contents, and applying learning from such study to new situations. Each Guide provides the following steps:

Step 1: Lesson Overview

This section provides a high-level summary of the lesson, culled from the video, lesson plans, and artifacts, to provide readers with some background information about the Instructional Set. Many include pre-observation notes in addition to the lesson plans. All lessons are based on rigorous student standards such as the Common Core State Standards (CCSS)/College and Career Readiness Anchor (CCRA) Standards.

Step 2: Preparation and Questions

Users examine artifacts that the teacher provided as evidence of preparing the lesson. The planning artifacts in an Instructional Set will include the lesson plans and related artifacts such as student assignments, if appropriate. Examining the planning artifacts and jotting down what to look for will help prepare users for viewing the video of the classroom lesson. Users will also generate questions that they have about the artifacts and use those questions when discussing the lesson with their colleagues.

Step 3: Viewing the Classroom Video

Users view the video of the full lesson and note significant behaviors of the teacher and students. Some of the Instructional Sets include samples of student work. The samples were selected by the teacher and do not include teacher comments. If student work is included, users will review it after viewing the video.

Step 4: Selected Highlights of the Lesson Video

This step provides a summary of important teacher and student behaviors that happened in the lesson, and which aspects of the teaching and learning are being exemplified. These noteworthy behaviors will provide users with a lens for their examination of the lesson with their colleagues, and an opportunity to match the highlights with the FFT Clusters.

Step 5: Viewing the Teacher Commentary

Users watch the video of the teacher commentary about the lesson and the students, and jot down noteworthy information. A summary of the commentary and its relationship to effective aspects of teaching are provided.

Step 6: Questions, Applications, and Discussion

Prompts are provided that guide users in analyzing and reflecting on the Instructional Set. This step also includes a set of prompts for thinking about applications to a user's own practice.

Using the Study Guides

The power of professional learning comes when educators can have focused discussions about the teaching and learning that they witness. Individuals can use the Study Guides, but the process of discussing with colleagues what one has learned from the Instructional Set, and how it can be applied to one's own practice, is the action needed to enhance teaching and learning. Just watching videos of effective teachers is not enough to change practice. Additional thinking and actions are needed to effect change. Therefore, the Study Guides are intended for use by educators participating in professional learning communities.

The Guides can be used in any order, but it is recommended that users begin with a grade level and subject area with which they are comfortable.

There are two versions in each Study Guide: one for communities of teachers and one for communities of instructional coaches or mentors of teachers. The first five steps of the process are identical in both versions, and are designed to focus on examining the instruction. A group setting is not necessary for Steps 1–5. They can be completed at an individual's own pace.

Steps 1–5 could be completed as a whole group, though this is not recommended, since interaction is not part of these steps. Watching a 45-minute video is usually best done as an individual activity so the viewer can control the pacing and the volume or elect to wear headphones.

Step 6 requires participants to share their responses, observations, suggestions, and other insights. It is highly recommended that participants work in small groups, so all get an opportunity to contribute to the discussions. The facilitator could select highlights of the small group discussions to share with the whole group.

Step 6 is a group activity, focusing on analyses of the Instructional Set and applications of learning. The activities in Step

6 are similar in the two versions, but the discussions will be different in subtle ways because of the user's role.

Teachers	Instructional Coaches
Communities with all teachers will analyze and reflect on the Instructional Set in Step 6 and will identify an aspect of the learning that went well and another aspect that could be improved. Their colleagues in the community will discuss the analyses and suggest teaching techniques to support student learning as related to the featured lesson. After that activity, the teacher community will think about what they learned from the teacher and lesson, and how they might apply that learning to their own teaching.	*Communities with all coaches/mentors will analyze the Instructional Set in Step 6 and discuss how to prepare for a conversation with the featured teacher. Their colleagues in the community will discuss the analyses and planned questions, comments, and suggestions. Step 6 includes an activity that has the coaches thinking about what they learned from the teacher and lesson, and how they might apply it to their own coaching situation.*

There may be communities comprising educators with different roles, such as a combination of teachers, teacher leaders, and a mentor of beginning teachers. The prompts in Step 6 can be easily modified to accommodate their different roles. There also might be situations where the professional development is done in a whole group setting. Just as with the mixed group learning communities, the prompts and implementation can be modified to support the professional development of all participants.

The Study Guides should be treated as one possible way of using the Instructional Sets for professional growth among educational colleagues. The Guides do not advocate any particular model of coaching or professional learning. If practitioners have a certain model that is used in their district, then they should consider modifying Step 6 to meet their needs or requirements. Additional prompts or steps can be included to support their learning and accommodate their schedules.

Post-Study Activities

Learning communities are encouraged to use the Study Guides as a springboard for creating their own additional professional development activities.

The following example shows an additional set of prompts that could be completed after the learning community completes the activities in Step 6 of the Guide. It serves as a reflective activity and should be done by individuals, then shared with their colleagues.

Here's What, So What, Now What

    a. Here's What: Identify five takeaways from your conversations with your colleagues. What examples did you collect?

    b. *So What:*   How do your takeaways connect to your current practice?

    c. *Now What:*   Based on the takeaways, identify 1–3 next steps you will take to inform your future practice.

Connection to the FFT Clusters

The Study Guides provide information and instructions on how to examine teaching and learning through the lens of the Framework for Teaching (FFT) Clusters. There are three versions of the FFT Clusters document: Generic, Literacy (ELA), and Mathematics. The Generic version reflects those instructional practices that are common across disciplines and was used for these Study Guides. The Literacy and Mathematics versions translate the general language of the narratives and critical attributes, where appropriate, into content-specific language.

Steps 1, 4, and 5 (lesson overview, lesson highlights, and teacher commentary) contain specific information about the Instructional Set and include prompts to match evidence to the related FFT Clusters. It is strongly suggested that copies of the FFT Clusters be available for participants so they can use them during their work with the Study Guides.

Even though the Guides were created with the FFT Clusters in mind, they also can be used to examine the Instructional Sets through the lens of the components of the Framework for Teaching. Practitioners who are familiar with the Framework for Teaching components will find the crosswalk between the Clusters and the components useful. It is located at the beginning of the FFT Clusters document. The FFT Clusters document can be downloaded for free individual use from the Danielson Group website: www.danielsongroup.org.

If practitioners use a different set of teaching standards than the Framework, they will still find the Study Guides and Instructional Sets useful for their professional growth needs. A crosswalk between their teaching standards and the FFT Clusters should be done so practitioners can associate the evidence in the Instructional Sets with their own standards.

Before you begin your examination of an Instructional Set's materials, you may want to check your equipment to make sure you can access the video and artifacts included with the Instructional Set. Enjoy studying the teaching and learning in the Instructional Set, and be prepared to enhance your own practice.

Looking at Teaching Through the Lens of the FFT Clusters

A Study Guide for
Teacher
Learning Communities

Teacher: Eisenman

Subject: ELA

Grade: 12

Topic: Evidence Based Analysis:
Hamlet's State of Mind

Welcome to the Study Guide for the Eisenman ELA Instructional Set, a collection of artifacts and videos for an instructional lesson. This Study Guide provides information and instructions on how to examine teaching and learning through the lens of the Framework for Teaching (FFT) Clusters. In order to complete the steps in this Guide, you will need access to the teacher's planning documents, the lesson video, and the teacher commentary video (http://www.danielsongroup.org/study-guides/). Steps 1–5 of this Study Guide focus on examining the Instructional Set and can be done by an individual. Step 6 is a group activity and focuses on sharing results of the analysis and applications of learning.

Step 1 - Lesson Overview

Read the background information of the lesson provided below.

This lesson consists of a whole-group discussion and a partner activity using a Shakespearean soliloquy. The class is using Hamlet's soliloquy, "Tis Now the Very Witching Time of Night" (Act 2, Scene 2), focusing on the pattern of diction and imagery to understand how characters evolve and change through a text. The lines to "Tis Now the Very Witching Time of Night" are provided by the teacher in the Interview Protocol for a Pre-Observation Conference. This text was selected because it is an important soliloquy that can help students understand a character's (in this case, Hamlet's chaotic) mental state. The students have previously studied soliloquies in terms of understanding the plot of a play. At the beginning of class, the teacher and students discuss in whole group the previous day's lesson and homework of watching the *Hamlet* video. This discussion connects student's previous day's learning to today's lesson.

The students are to copy the text of "Tis Now the Very Witching Hour" on chart paper in a partner activity, leaving a blank line after each punctuation mark. On these blank lines, the paired students analyze Hamlet's words and write at least 12 responses to Hamlet, changing the soliloquy into a dialogue. The students are to pretend Horatio, Hamlet's friend, is still in the room with Hamlet. They are to create 12 original interpolated questions or comments that Horatio will speak to Hamlet, and write the new interpolated dialogue on the poster. The students are to rehearse their new dialogue after they complete the poster, and be prepared to perform this for the class.

One outcome of the lesson is to help students predict what will happen in future scenes. The students should be able at the end of the lesson to determine Hamlet's mental state and predict if he will do harm to his mother in upcoming scenes.

Step 2 - Preparation and Questions

- *Read the teacher's lesson plan and jot down things you expect to see and what you want to look for in the video of the lesson.*

- *Write down any questions or comments you have about the lesson plan.*

Step 3 – Viewing the Classroom Video

- *View the complete video, noting those things you expected to see based on the lesson plan. Also note what was missing based on your expectations from the lesson plan. Jot down significant behaviors by the teacher and students pertinent to the FFT Clusters.*

Step 4 – Selected Highlights of the Lesson Video

Read the highlights of the lesson provided below. Note those matching your highlights of the lesson. For each set of statements, determine the FFT Cluster that is best related to the behaviors presented.

Ms. Eisenman has designed a lesson that incorporates productive struggle by challenging the students to be accountable for their own learning throughout the class period. She requires students to use one another as resources and to use an iPad to discover the meaning of words from the Shakespearean era using an online version of the Oxford English Dictionary. Students persevere throughout the lesson.

> A. *The teacher asks for volunteers to share their presentations. Four different sets of partners share. They visibly care about their work. One group writes very humorous comments that Hamlet's friend might make to him. The teacher says, "I'm enjoying your sarcasm." The teacher and students listen with respect and respond positively during presentations. Students applaud politely after each presentation. The students' actions and comments show they feel safe to use humor on their chart and enjoy having their efforts respected by both their peers and teacher. (Cluster ____)*

B. *Most of the partner work appears to be divided equally between pairs. One writes, one looks up definitions in the Oxford English Dictionary; both discuss. Some share the task of writing also. (Cluster ___)*

C. *Students demonstrate perseverance and tolerance toward one another as they work together in partners to try to discern the meaning of Shakespeare's words. For example, some random comments observed:*
   - *S: I don't understand the "soft" part here? What does he mean?*
   - *T: Look at the punctuation.*
   - *S1: I don't get that word. Could you look it up? S2: It means disgraced. S1: Oh, so he is like ashamed of her?*
   - *S: I love that line. Your soul is messed up.*
   - *S: I think he's just pretending to be crazy.*
   - *S: Why would he do that? It is a soliloquy. Who is he trying to convince? He is the only one there.*
   - *S: He is really leaning toward crazy here.*
   - *S: But she is his mom. Everyone gets mad at their mom, but moms deserve respect. (Cluster ___)*

D. *Desks are arranged in sets of two before the lesson so that the transition to working with partners is very smooth. There is no loss of instructional time for moving desks, since the teacher assigned the students to partner with the person sitting beside them. Students pass out markers of two different colors while the teacher distributes chart papers. (Cluster ___)*

E. *Pictures of authors (including Shakespeare) and characters from books are displayed on the walls. Supplies, iPads, and books are accessible. Students have iPads on their desks when the observation begins. Each pair of students has access to at least one iPad. During the teacher commentary, there are many books and materials visible that can be used to support literacy. Supplies seem to be well-organized and accessible to students. (Cluster ___)*

F. *The teacher poses higher-level thinking questions that challenge students to form hypotheses during both the full class discussion and the partner discussion. As students work together to discover the meaning behind Hamlet's words, the teacher circulates and monitors by asking such questions as:*
   - *What do you think is going on in his head?*
   - *What does he mean by that? Use evidence but tell me in your own words.*
   - *What would you say to him if he were your best friend?*
   - *Do Hamlet's words help you predict what will happen in the next acts of this play? (Cluster ___)*

G. *The teacher engages students by making the partner activity both challenging and fun. She has students pretend Horatio is still with Hamlet, and create their own 12 original interruptions that Horatio might say. (18:58) T: Guys listen. You don't have to be so serious…hot blood? How about hot chocolate? (Cluster ___)*

H. *The teacher takes another finger survey following the partner activity and presentations.*
   - *T: What do you think about Hamlet's emotional state now?*
   - *S: He's indecisive, his tone, crazy, talking to himself.*
   - *T: There is a change, right?*
   - *S: He starts off talking with negative words and ends with him being more positive… gets less intense as we read it.*
   - *S (John): Battling against himself, angels and demons on his shoulders. At the beginning of the story angel, pure; after scene two, changes more to the devil, darker sides of Hamlet. (Cluster ___)*

I. *T (in closing): Last thing I would like you to do with your partner is make a prediction based on the soliloquy and your writings. What is Hamlet going to do in the upcoming scenes? Cite evidence to support that. (The lesson plan notes that the students will be turning in these responses.) (Cluster ___)*

Step 5 – Viewing the Teacher Commentary

Watch the video of the teacher's commentary about the lesson and jot down any questions or comments you have about the commentary. Read the highlights below and identify the related FFT Cluster.

A. Ms. Eisenman states that students have previously looked at soliloquies in terms of understanding the plot of a play when she shares the background of the topic (Evidence Based Analysis—Hamlet's State of Mind). She planned for students to dig further into the craft and construction of a soliloquy in this lesson. She chose soliloquies because they frequently reveal a character's mental state. (Cluster ___)

B. Ms. Eisenman, when reflecting about the success of the lesson, says that students used evidence to build on each other's observations and insights. She explains that having partners promoted conversations and the sharing of ideas. She says that the students encouraged one another to find and use textual evidence. Mrs. Eisenman notes that doing all the activities gave students greater understanding into Hamlet's mental state. (Cluster ___)

Step 6 – Questions, Applications, and Discussion

The purpose of this step is to prompt your analysis and reflection of the Instructional Set and to have you think about applications to your own practice.

1. **Teaching and Learning Related to the FFT Clusters**
The purpose of the activity is to increase your understanding of the relationship between the highlights of the Instructional Set

and the FFT Clusters. Your identification of an FFT Cluster for each of the highlights is compared to the Cluster identified by the master coders. The Answer Key is located at the end of the activities. You have options on how to complete the comparison. Determine what might work best for your group's learning. Options include, but are not limited to the following.

- Look at the first set of highlights. Take a poll of what each group member identified as the related FFT Cluster. If all members said the same FFT Cluster, have one or two members say why. Compare the group's response to the answer sheet. Repeat for the remainder of the highlights.

OR

- Have each member take one or two highlights. State the correct answer for each one, and a reason why the highlight demonstrates that FFT Cluster. The member will facilitate a discussion if others had different responses, with the goal of having all understand the justification of the correct answer.

OR

- Have members check their own responses to all the highlights. If there are any incorrect answers, then the member selects one highlight and leads a discussion with the group to learn why others think the highlight matches the correct FFT Cluster.

OR

- Determine your own process to check and discuss the match between highlights and the FFT Clusters.

2. Analysis and Reflection of the Instructional Set

The purpose of this activity is for you to analyze and reflect on what you saw and heard in the artifacts and videos, to share your analysis with your peers, and to discuss some of the questions or comments you noted. Review the notes, comments, and questions you recorded when you examined the Instructional Set.

- Identify a key teaching and learning attribute demonstrated in the Instructional Set that was effective and state why you think it worked well.

- Identify a different attribute and provide ideas about how it could be enhanced or improved.

- Share your statements with your group and have your peers react to and build upon your analysis and ideas.

Sample statements:

I noticed that the teacher was successful in getting the students to participate in the discussion during both the whole group and partner activities throughout the lesson. The students consistently raised their hands during whole group class discussions, and waited to be called upon to explain their thinking and cite evidence. The teacher served as a facilitator, orchestrating student interactions. Based on the level of the students' participation during the discussions, the students may be at the point where they could assume more of a facilitator role: to ask questions of other students or offer comments directly. I know this often presents something of a challenge for teachers. A possible strategy to begin this transition might be to identify students in the class who, if given the prompt, would ask questions directly to their peers.

Additional ideas for statements:

- Degree to which students take pride in their work and demonstrate a commitment to mastering challenging content

- Extent to which the instructional strategies used by the teacher are appropriate for the discipline

- Extent to which students monitor their own learning and provide feedback to others

- Extent to which the teacher provides wait time following questions, allowing students time to think and to construct an answer

3. **Notice, Learn, and Apply**

The purpose of this activity is for you to reflect on what you learned from your analysis of the Instructional Set and to determine how you will apply it to your teaching.

- Complete the statements:
  "I noticed _____."
  (Insert one thing you noticed about the teacher or students.)

  "And I learned _____."
  (State what you learned related to what you noticed.)

  "I will apply what I learned by _____."
  (Provide example of how you will use what you learned in your own context.)

- Share your statements with your group. Have others react and add how they might apply what you noticed to their own teaching context.

Sample statement:

- I noticed during whole-class discussions, the conversations were teacher-to-student or student-to-teacher and not student-to-student.

- I learned that even though the students understood the content, they would need prompting and even encouragement to take on a facilitator role.

- I will apply what I learned by allowing my students to take on this role. Since facilitating a discussion with a whole class might be intimidating for a student, I will place them in small groups and assign one student in the group the role of facilitator. I will provide the questions or prompts they will use to start the discussion, but it will be up to them to keep the discussion going.

Study Guide for Teachers Answer Key

Highlights from the Lesson Video (Step 4)

A. The teacher asks for volunteers to share their presentations. Four different sets of partners share. They visibly care about their work. One group writes very humorous comments that Hamlet's friend might make to him. The teacher says, "I'm enjoying your sarcasm." The teacher and students listen with respect and respond positively during presentations.... (Cluster 2 Safe, Respectful, Supportive, and Challenging Learning Environment)

B. Most of the partner work appears to be divided equally between pairs. One writes, one looks up definitions in the Oxford English Dictionary; both discuss. Some share the task of writing also. (Cluster 2 Safe, Respectful, Supportive, and Challenging Learning Environment)

C. Students demonstrate perseverance and tolerance toward one another as they work together in partners to try to discern the meaning of Shakespeare's words. For example, some random comments observed: S: I don't understand the "soft" part here? What does he mean... (Cluster 2 Safe, Respectful, Supportive, and Challenging Learning Environment)

D. Desks are arranged in sets of two before the lesson so that the transition to working with partners is very smooth. There is no loss of instructional time for moving desks, since the teacher assigned the students to partner with the person sitting beside them. Students pass out markers of two different colors while the teacher distributes chart papers. (Cluster 3 Classroom Management)

E. Pictures of authors (including Shakespeare) and characters from books are displayed on the walls. Supplies, iPads, and books are accessible. Students have iPads on their desks when the observation begins. Each pair of students has access to at least one iPad. During the teacher commentary, there are many books and materials visible... (Cluster 3 Classroom Management)

F. The teacher poses higher-level thinking questions that challenge students to form hypotheses during both the full class discussion and the partner discussion. As students work together to discover the meaning behind Hamlet's words, the teacher circulates and monitors by asking such questions as: What do you think is going on in his head?... (Cluster 4 Student Intellectual Engagement)

G. The teacher engages students by making the partner activity both challenging and fun. She has students pretend Horatio is still with Hamlet, and create their own 12 original interruptions that Horatio might say. (18:58) T: Guys listen. You don't have to be so serious...hot blood? How about hot chocolate. (Cluster 4 Student Intellectual Engagement)

H. *The teacher takes another finger survey following the partner activity and presentations.*
   - *T: What do you think about Hamlet's emotional state now?*
   - *S: He's indecisive, his tone, crazy, talking to himself.*
   - *T: There is a change, right?*

Study Guide for Teachers Answer Key

Highlights from the Lesson Video (Step 4)

- *S: He starts off talking with negative words and ends with him being more positive... gets less intense as we read it.*
- *S (John): Battling against himself, angels and demons on his shoulders. At the beginning of the story angel, pure; after scene two, changes more to the devil, darker sides of Hamlet.* (Cluster 5 Successful Learning by All Students)

I. *T (in closing): Last thing I would like you to do with your partner is make a prediction based on the soliloquy and your writings. What is Hamlet going to do in the upcoming scenes? Cite evidence to support that. (The lesson plan notes that the students will be turning in these responses.)* (Cluster 5 Successful Learning by All Students)

Study Guide for Teachers Answer Key

Highlights from the Teacher Commentary (Step 5)

A. Ms. Eisenman states that students have previously looked at soliloquies in terms of understanding the plot of a play when she shares the background of the topic (Evidence Based Analysis – Hamlet's State of Mind). She planned for students to dig further into the craft and construction of a soliloquy in this lesson. She chose soliloquies because they frequently reveal a character's mental state. (Cluster 1 Clarity of Instructional Purpose and Accuracy of Content)

B. Ms. Eisenman, when reflecting about the success of the lesson, says that students used evidence to build on each other's observations and insights. She explains that having partners promoted conversations and the sharing of ideas. She says that the students encouraged one another to find and use textual evidence. Mrs. Eisenman notes that doing all the activities gave students greater understanding into Hamlet's mental state. (Cluster 5 Successful Learning by All Students)

**Looking at Teaching Through
the Lens of the FFT Clusters**

A Study Guide for
Instructional Coach
Learning Communities

Teacher: Eisenman
Subject: ELA
Grade: 12
Topic: Evidence Based Analysis:
Hamlet's State of Mind

Welcome to the Study Guide for the Eisenman ELA Instructional Set, a collection of artifacts and videos for an instructional lesson. This Study Guide provides information and instructions on how to examine teaching and learning through the lens of the Framework for Teaching (FFT) Clusters. In order to complete the steps in this Guide, you will need access to the teacher's planning documents, the lesson video, and the teacher commentary video (http://www.danielsongroup.org/study-guides/). Steps 1–5 of this Study Guide focus on examining the Instructional Set and can be done by an individual. Step 6 is a group activity and focuses on sharing results of the analysis and applications of learning.

Step 1 - Lesson Overview

Read the background information of the lesson provided below.

This lesson consists of a whole-group discussion and a partner activity using a Shakespearean soliloquy. The class is using Hamlet's soliloquy, "Tis Now the Very Witching Time of Night" (Act 2 Scene 2) to understand how characters evolve and change through a text, especially when focusing on the pattern of diction and imagery. The lines to "Tis Now the Very Witching Time of Night" are provided by the teacher in the Interview Protocol for a Pre-Observation Conference. This text was selected because it is an important soliloquy that can help students understand a character's (in this case, Hamlet's chaotic) mental state. The students have previously studied soliloquies in terms of understanding the plot of a play. At the beginning of class, the teacher and students discuss in whole group the previous day's lesson and homework of watching the *Hamlet* video. This discussion connects student's previous day's learning to today's lesson.

The students in a partner activity are to copy the text of "Tis Now the Very Witching Hour" on chart paper, leaving a blank line after each punctuation mark. On these blank lines, the paired students analyze Hamlet's words and write at least 12 responses to Hamlet, changing the soliloquy into a dialogue. The students are to pretend Horatio, Hamlet's friend, is still in the room with Hamlet. They are to create 12 original interpolated questions or comments that Horatio will speak to Hamlet, and write the new interpolated dialogue on the poster. After the students complete the poster, they are to rehearse together their new dialogue and be prepared to perform this for the class.

One outcome of the lesson is to help students predict what will happen in future scenes. The students should be able at the end of the lesson to determine Hamlet's mental state and predict if he will do harm to his mother in upcoming scenes.

Step 2 - Preparation and Questions

- *Read the teacher's lesson plan and jot down things you expect to see and what you want to look for in the video of the lesson.*

- *Write down any questions or comments you have about the lesson plan.*

Step 3 – Viewing the Classroom Video

- *View the complete video, noting those things you expected to see based on the lesson plan. Also note what was missing based on your expectations from the lesson plan. Jot down significant behaviors by the teacher and students pertinent to the FFT Clusters.*

Step 4 – Selected Highlights of the Lesson Video

Read the highlights of the lesson provided below. Note those matching your highlights of the lesson. For each set of statements, determine the FFT Cluster that is best related to the behaviors presented.

Ms. Eisenman has designed a lesson in which productive struggle is used by challenging the students to be accountable for their own learning throughout the class period. She requires students to use one another as resources and to use an iPad to discover the meaning of words from the Shakespearean era using an online version of the Oxford English Dictionary. Students persevere throughout the lesson.

> A. *The teacher asks for volunteers to share their presentations. Four different sets of partners share. They visibly care about their work. One group writes very humorous comments that Hamlet's friend might make to him. The teacher says, "I'm enjoying your sarcasm." The teacher and students listen with respect and respond positively during presentations. Students applaud politely after each presentation. The students' actions and comments show they feel safe to use humor on their chart and enjoy having their efforts respected by both their peers and teacher. (Cluster ____)*

B. *Most of the partner work appears to be divided equally between pairs. One writes, one looks up definitions in the Oxford English Dictionary; both discuss. Some share the task of writing also. (Cluster ___)*

C. *Students demonstrate perseverance and tolerance toward one another as they work together in partners to try to discern the meaning of Shakespeare's words. For example, some random comments observed:*
   - *S: I don't understand the "soft" part here? What does he mean?*
   - *T: Look at the punctuation.*
   - *S1: I don't get that word. Could you look it up? S2: It means disgraced. S1: Oh, so he is like ashamed of her?*
   - *S: I love that line. Your soul is messed up.*
   - *S: I think he's just pretending to be crazy.*
   - *S: Why would he do that? It is a soliloquy. Who is he trying to convince? He is the only one there.*
   - *S: He is really leaning toward crazy here.*
   - *S: But she is his mom. Everyone gets mad at their mom, but moms deserve respect. (Cluster ___)*

D. *Desks are arranged in sets of two before the lesson so that the transition to working with partners is very smooth. There is no loss of instructional time for moving desks, since the teacher assigned the students to partner with the person sitting beside them. Students pass out markers of two different colors while the teacher distributes chart papers. (Cluster ___)*

E. *Pictures of authors (including Shakespeare) and characters from books are displayed on the walls. Supplies, iPads, and books are accessible. Students have iPads on their desks when the observation begins. Each pair of students has access to at least one iPad. During the teacher commentary, there are many books and materials visible that can be used to support literacy. Supplies seem to be well-organized and accessible to students. (Cluster ___)*

F. *The teacher poses higher-level thinking questions that challenge students to form hypotheses during both the full class discussion and the partner discussion. As stu-*

dents work together to discover the meaning behind Hamlet's words, the teacher circulates and monitors by asking such questions as:

- What do you think is going on in his head?
- What does he mean by that? Use evidence but tell me in your own words.
- What would you say to him if he were your best friend?
- Do Hamlet's words help you predict what will happen in the next acts of this play? (Cluster ___)

G. The teacher engages students by making the partner activity both challenging and fun. She has students pretend Horatio is still with Hamlet, and create their own 12 original interruptions that Horatio might say. (18:58) T: Guys listen. You don't have to be so serious...hot blood? How about hot chocolate? (Cluster ___)

H. The teacher takes another finger survey following the partner activity and presentations.

- T: What do you think about Hamlet's emotional state now?
- S: He's indecisive, his tone, crazy, talking to himself.
- T: There is a change, right?
- S: He starts off talking with negative words and ends with him being more positive... gets less intense as we read it.
- S (John): Battling against himself, angels and demons on his shoulders. At the beginning of the story angel, pure; after scene two, changes more to the devil, darker sides of Hamlet. (Cluster ___)

I. T (in closing): Last thing I would like you to do with your partner is make a prediction based on the soliloquy and your writings. What is Hamlet going to do in the upcoming scenes? Cite evidence to support that. (The lesson plan notes that the students will be turning in these responses.) (Cluster ___)

Step 5 – Viewing the Teacher Commentary

Watch the video of the teacher's commentary about the lesson and jot down any questions or comments you have about the commentary. Read the highlights below and identify the related FFT Cluster.

A. Ms. Eisenman states that students have previously looked at soliloquies in terms of understanding the plot of a play when she shares the background of the topic (Evidence Based Analysis—Hamlet's State of Mind). She planned for students to dig further into the craft and construction of a soliloquy in this lesson. She chose soliloquies because they frequently reveal a character's mental state. (Cluster ___)

B. Ms. Eisenman, when reflecting about the success of the lesson, says that students used evidence to build on each other's observations and insights. She explains that having partners promoted conversations and the sharing of ideas. She says that the students encouraged one another to find and use textual evidence. Mrs. Eisenman notes that doing all the activities gave students greater understanding into Hamlet's mental state. (Cluster ___)

Step 6 – Questions, Applications, and Discussion

The purpose of this step is to prompt your analysis and reflection of the Instructional Set and to have you think about applications to your own practice.

1. **Teaching and Learning Related to the FFT Clusters**

The purpose of the activity is to increase your understanding of the relationship between the highlights of the Instructional Set and the FFT Clusters. Your identification of an FFT Cluster for each of the highlights is compared to the Cluster identified by the master coders. The Answer Key is located at the end of the activities. You have options on how to complete the comparison. Determine what might work best for your group's learning. Options include, but are not limited to the following.

- Look at the first set of highlights. Take a poll of what each group member identified as the related FFT Cluster. If all members said the same FFT Cluster, then have one or two members say why. Compare the group's response to the answer sheet. Repeat for the remainder of the sets of highlights.

OR

- Have each member take one or two sets of highlights and be the discussant for them. The discussant will state the correct answer and state a reason why the statements in the set demonstrate the FFT Cluster. The discussant will facilitate a discussion if members had different responses with the goal of all understanding the justification of the correct answer.

OR

- Have members check their own responses to all the sets of highlights. If there are any incorrect answers, then the member selects one set and leads a discussion with the group to learn why others think the highlights match the correct FFT Cluster.

OR

- Determine your own process to check and discuss the match between highlights and the FFT Clusters.

2. Analysis and Reflection of the Instructional Set

The purpose of this activity is for you to analyze and reflect on what you saw and heard in the artifacts and videos and to discuss some of the questions or comments you noted. One element of a professional conversation is asking questions to ascertain more information about a teacher's thinking and the behaviors of both students and teacher. This activity allows you and your peers to practice preparing such questions. Your peers can comment on whether your questions are appropriate and will obtain useful information without making the featured teacher feel uneasy or criticized.

The second part of this activity focuses on helping teachers move their practice forward. Please note that having you prepare for and model an entire conversation about the lesson with the featured teacher is not the purpose of this activity as written. Your group can modify or replace the activity to meet your group's needs

- Review the notes, comments, and questions you recorded when you examined the Instructional Set. Pretend you have the opportunity to ask the teacher some questions to get additional information about the strategies used or decisions made for this Instructional Set.

- Share with your group just the questions you would use with the teacher to elicit additional information. Have your peers comment about your questions and add other questions they had about the same event.

- Share with others in your group what you would do to prompt the teacher's thinking and actions to enhance his/her practice. Take turns sharing and discussing the prompts.

Sample A, Part I:

Ms. Eisenman, I would like to take a few moments to discuss how you gave directions to students for the summative assessment. You were very clear in the instructions you provided: "Last thing I would like you to do with your partner is make a prediction based on the soliloquy and your writings. What is Hamlet going to do in the upcoming scenes? Cite evidence to support that." Also, you noted in your lesson plan that the partners would be turning in their responses. Based on the responses of the class as a whole, were there any particular areas of success or weakness you noticed about their predictions? For those who were successful with their predictions, are there any examples that come to mind that led you to this conclusion? As for those partners who may have not been as successful as others, what were some of the areas of weakness you noted for these students? What might be some plans or ideas you have in mind for strengthening their understanding of this lesson?

Sample A, Part II:

I noticed the students had about two minutes to complete the summative assessment. For those students who may not have finished within the time period, what were some options they had for completing the task? In reflecting on your lesson outline, what might be some things you would consider changing to allow students more time to complete the summative assessment?

Sample B, Part I:

I observed that students consistently stayed on task throughout most of the partner activity. With the exception of one set of partners, the work appeared to be divided equally between pairs; with one student writing while the other student looked up definitions in the Oxford English Dictionary. Some shared the writing also. The exception was the boy in the gray shirt sitting next to the girl in the yellow and black shirt. I observed the girl doing most of the work. Your lesson plan mentioned two students with 504 plans who may need extended time. You also mentioned grouping the students heterogeneously to assist students with greater needs. Do either of these planning elements refer to this pair of partners? Can you happen to recall how they did on their summative assessment? (If the teacher shares the pair didn't do well, I would ask: What might be some plans or ideas you have in mind to do next for this pair of students or others who also did not do well?)

Sample B, Part II:

Ms. Eisenman, you are to be commended for cognitively engaging your students throughout the lesson. In reflecting on your lesson outline and planning, what are some areas you think went really well? If you were going to reteach this lesson, can you share any changes you would want to make?

3. **Notice, Learn, and Apply**

The purpose of this activity is for you to reflect on what you learned from your analysis of the Instructional Set and to determine how you will apply it to your teaching.

- Complete the statements:
  "I noticed _____."
  (Insert one thing you noticed about the teacher or students.)

  "And I learned _____."
  (State what you learned related to what you noticed.)

  "I will apply what I learned by _____."
  (Provide example of how you will use what you learned in your own context.)

- Share your statements with your group. Have others react and add how they might apply what you noticed to their own coaching context.

Sample statements:

- I noticed during the teacher commentary video and the "Interview Protocol for a Pre-Observation (Planning) Conference" document, Ms. Eisenman made no suggestions for improving her lesson.

- I learned that in pre-planning for the conference, it is important for the coach to prepare questions that will cause the teacher to reflect on both her teaching as well as the students' learning during the lesson.

- I will apply what I learned by preparing questions before the interview for any areas of improvement I wish to discuss with the teacher based on evidence collected during the observation.

FFT Clusters Study Guide: Set 4 (ELA 12)

Study Guide for Teachers Answer Key

Highlights from the Lesson Video (Step 4)

A. The teacher asks for volunteers to share their presentations. Four different sets of partners share. They visibly care about their work. One group writes very humorous comments that Hamlet's friend might make to him. The teacher says, "I'm enjoying your sarcasm." The teacher and students listen with respect and respond positively during presentations.... (Cluster 2 Safe, Respectful, Supportive, and Challenging Learning Environment)

B. Most of the partner work appears to be divided equally between pairs. One writes, one looks up definitions in the Oxford English Dictionary; both discuss. Some share the task of writing also. (Cluster 2 Safe, Respectful, Supportive, and Challenging Learning Environment)

C. Students demonstrate perseverance and tolerance toward one another as they work together in partners to try to discern the meaning of Shakespeare's words. For example, some random comments observed: S: I don't understand the "soft" part here? What does he mean... (Cluster 2 Safe, Respectful, Supportive, and Challenging Learning Environment)

D. Desks are arranged in sets of two before the lesson so that the transition to working with partners is very smooth. There is no loss of instructional time for moving desks, since the teacher assigned the students to partner with the person sitting beside them. Students pass out markers of two different colors while the teacher distributes chart papers. (Cluster 3 Classroom Management)

E. Pictures of authors (including Shakespeare) and characters from books are displayed on the walls. Supplies, iPads, and books are accessible. Students have iPads on their desks when the observation begins. Each pair of students has access to at least one iPad. During the teacher commentary, there are many books and materials visible... (Cluster 3 Classroom Management)

F. The teacher poses higher-level thinking questions that challenge students to form hypotheses during both the full class discussion and the partner discussion. As students work together to discover the meaning behind Hamlet's words, the teacher circulates and monitors by asking such questions as: What do you think is going on in his head?... (Cluster 4 Student Intellectual Engagement)

G. The teacher engages students by making the partner activity both challenging and fun. She has students pretend Horatio is still with Hamlet, and create their own 12 original interruptions that Horatio might say. (18:58) T: Guys listen. You don't have to be so serious...hot blood? How about hot chocolate. (Cluster 4 Student Intellectual Engagement)

H. *The teacher takes another finger survey following the partner activity and presentations.*
   - *T: What do you think about Hamlet's emotional state now?*
   - *S: He's indecisive, his tone, crazy, talking to himself.*
   - *T: There is a change, right?*

Study Guide for Teachers Answer Key

Highlights from the Lesson Video (Step 4)

- S: He starts off talking with negative words and ends with him being more positive... gets less intense as we read it.
- S (John): Battling against himself, angels and demons on his shoulders. At the beginning of the story angel, pure; after scene two, changes more to the devil, darker sides of Hamlet. (Cluster 5 Successful Learning by All Students)

I. T (in closing): Last thing I would like you to do with your partner is make a prediction based on the soliloquy and your writings. What is Hamlet going to do in the upcoming scenes? Cite evidence to support that. (The lesson plan notes that the students will be turning in these responses.) (Cluster 5 Successful Learning by All Students)

Study Guide for Instructional Coaches Answer Key

Highlights from the Teacher Commentary (Step 5)

A. Ms. Eisenman states that students have previously looked at soliloquies in terms of understanding the plot of a play when she shares the background of the topic (Evidence Based Analysis – Hamlet's State of Mind). She planned for students to dig further into the craft and construction of a soliloquy in this lesson. She chose soliloquies because they frequently reveal a character's mental state. (Cluster 1 Clarity of Instructional Purpose and Accuracy of Content)

B. Ms. Eisenman, when reflecting about the success of the lesson, says that students used evidence to build on each other's observations and insights. She explains that having partners promoted conversations and the sharing of ideas. She says that the students encouraged one another to find and use textual evidence. Mrs. Eisenman notes that doing all the activities gave students greater understanding into Hamlet's mental state. (Cluster 5 Successful Learning by All Students)

Record of Evidence

This Record of Evidence (ROE) contains key evidence aligned to the FFT Clusters. Interpretive statements about the evidence are also provided. The ROE was created by two master coders who recorded evidence and interpretation statements independently, reviewed each others' work, and arrived at a final composite version based on their professional conversations. This version was reviewed by a leader of the master coders. The ROE is included in this Study Guide so users can see what master coders identified as key evidence, and their interpretation of that evidence through the lens of the FFT Clusters. It is provided as an example of one type of analysis of an Instructional Set. The ROEs were created for professional development rather than evaluative purposes. Users are cautioned about using them for teacher evaluation.

Rubric:	Generic
Grade:	12
Subject:	ELA
Topic:	Evidence Based Analysis: Hamlet's State of Mind
Teacher description:	Female, white, experience not provided
Class description:	Approximately 18 students in class. From lesson plan: "Most students in this class are reading and writing appropriately for grade level. One student in SRBI, two students have a 504 plan for extra time. There are 4–5 students who consistently perform above expectations. The remaining 12 students are average learners. This group is particularly very social. They like to talk. Hopefully this activity will allow them to socialize and still work on the task at hand."
Artifacts:	• Lesson plan
	• Interview Protocol for a Pre-observation Interview Conference
	• Hard copy of slide show containing Eisenman's interpolated comments and questions
	• Teacher commentary video
Length of video:	44:43

Record of Evidence

Cluster 1: Clarity of Instructional Purpose and Accuracy of Content

Guiding Questions

- *To what extent does the teacher demonstrate depth of important content knowledge and conduct the class with a clear and ambitious purpose, reflective of the standards for the discipline and appropriate to the students' levels of knowledge and skill?*

- *To what degree are the elements of a lesson (the sequence of topics, instructional strategies, and materials and resources) well designed and executed, and aligned with the purpose of the lesson?*

- *To what extent are they designed to engage students in high-level learning in the discipline?*

Evidence

Instructional Plan
- The lesson plan includes explanation of how the lesson will address:
  - The CCSS ELA/literacy standards
  - The words to "Tis Now the Witching Time of Night" soliloquy
  - Two learning outcomes
  - Materials to be used
  - Explanation of how this lesson fits in with previous and future learning
  - Explanation of how questions will be used to motivate students to use textual evidence and other resources to make predictions about Hamlet's mental state.
- The lesson plan also explains how the activities address Core Actions 1 and 2. They include a description of the class, including those with special needs; an explanation of how differentiation will be accomplished; and how the teacher will know if the students have learned what she intended.

Artifacts
- Interview Protocol for a Pre-Observation (Planning) Conference
- Copy of a slide show that includes teacher-interpolated comments and questions proposed for a previously-read soliloquy
- Teacher Commentary video

Teacher Commentary
- Teacher states that students have previously looked at soliloquies in terms of understanding the plot of a play. Teacher wants students to dig further into the craft and construction of a soliloquy. Teacher states in interview that soliloquies frequently reveal a character's mental state.
- Teacher's reflection:
  1. Students use their iPads constantly, which is different from the past.
  2. Students use evidence to build on each other's observations and insights.

Record of Evidence

Cluster 1:   Clarity of Instructional Purpose and Accuracy of Content

Evidence (cont'd.)

3. Being paired promotes conversations and sharing ideas.
4. Students encourage one another to find and use textual evidence.
5. Doing all the activities gives students greater understanding into Hamlet's mental state.

Video

- Teacher asks the students about their homework, briefly making a connection with the past lesson, and tying it to today's lesson. Teacher tells students that today's lesson will help them predict what will happen in the play in future scenes.
- Teacher has students assess Hamlet's current emotional state by doing a finger survey. She explains: "One finger means Hamlet is completely sane and five means crazy." Most students judge him to be a three but a couple think four. She calls on a few students to explain their ratings. Teacher reveals that they will repeat this survey after today's lesson.
- After an explanation of the activity, students are paired using heterogeneous grouping. The students write the lines of Shakespeare's soliloquy "Tis Now the Very Witching Hour" on chart paper. They leave a blank line between each line of the soliloquy. On this blank line, they talk to Hamlet as if they are his friend. They might ask him a question or make a comment to try and calm him.
- (4:45) T: "What is the definition of a soliloquy?" A couple of students answer, and teacher writes their definitions on the board. T: "Why do we use a soliloquy?" Students share ideas. Discussion continues until students suggest that soliloquies reveal the character's emotional state.
- The lesson plan states that students will orally read a previous soliloquy as a class with pauses at each punctuation mark. The teacher will interject a comment Horatio may have made in response to each line. Teacher will be modeling the activity for students to enhance their understanding of the task. Teacher makes no mention in the lesson plan of specific misconceptions the students may have. She addresses the fact this will be a challenging activity that will likely elicit a wide variety of responses. In the lesson plan, the teacher explains that students will determine Hamlet's mental state to be unstable, and they will predict he may do harm to his mother in upcoming scenes.
- The slide show prompts a discussion of the term soliloquy. It poses the question of why plays in Shakespeare's time included soliloquies. Teacher compares Shakespearean works to today's soap operas that include voice over comments that people in the scene can't hear, but which the viewer can. Teacher tells students that most of the time when we witness a soliloquy in a play, it tells us something about a character's emotional state. The slide show contains the dialogue of two soliloquies from *Hamlet*.

Record of Evidence

Cluster 1: Clarity of Instructional Purpose and Accuracy of Content

Evidence (cont'd.)

- Teacher gives the following directions to the students: "With your partner, you are to change Hamlet's soliloquy into a dialogue. You are to act like you are his friend. You are to interrupt him 12 times. Watch for the punctuation marks that will help you know when to interrupt. You may ask him questions about what he is saying or possibly say things to calm him down. Be his friend."
- While the students work with partners, the teacher circulates, asking and answering questions of partners and individuals, assessing their comprehension of the text.
- One male student, seated with the girl in the Sponge Bob shirt, seems to be doing not much work at all. Teacher notices his disengagement. She asks him to describe his role in his partnership. He says, "She's doing the writing." Teacher then encourages him to look up words for the first line. His participation improves.
- Four sets of partners present their charts in front of the class. Teacher frames this presentation as a competition and offers prizes. Class members participate in a quick secret vote on which presentation is the best.
- Students retake the finger survey ranking Hamlet's emotional state again. Many students have changed to four or five following their partner activity.
- Summative assignment: Teacher tells students to write on the back of the chart paper and make a prediction about what will happen next in the play, and to add the evidence they use for that prediction.
- Video ends with the bell ringing. The students' written predictions with their evidence for the closing task are not available to the observers.

Record of Evidence

Cluster 1: **Clarity of Instructional Purpose and Accuracy of Content**

Interpretation

- *There are appropriate learning goals that align with CCSS. Detailed activities and questions are appropriate and scaffold the learning objectives.*
- *No content errors are noted in the plan or delivery of the lesson.*
- *The teacher's plans and interview do not address any anticipated misconceptions the students may have. Teacher mentions intra-disciplinary connections, but connections to other disciplines are not observed.*
- *The teacher plans and uses formative assessments throughout the lesson.*
- *Ms. Eisenman orally reads only a few lines from a previous soliloquy and her interpolations before she asks the students to begin working. Following the lesson plan might have helped the students build comprehension for the material and the task.*
- *Teacher circulates and monitors students' engagement.*
- *Students have time following their presentations to reflect during a closing discussion.*
- *Students have less than two minutes to write their predictions before the bell rings.*
- *The availability of some of the students' responses on the summative assessment may have further substantiated the lesson's effectiveness.*

Record of Evidence

Cluster 2: Safe, Respectful, Supportive, and Challenging Learning Environment

Guiding Questions

- *To what extent do the interactions between teacher and students, and among students, demonstrate genuine caring and a safe, respectful, supportive, and also challenging learning environment?*

- *Do teachers convey high expectations for student learning and encourage hard work and perseverance? Is the environment safe for risk taking?*

- *Do students take pride in their work and demonstrate a commitment to mastering challenging content?*

Evidence

- A long narrow poster on the wall says, "Strive for Excellence."

- Teacher conveys high expectations for student learning from the very beginning to the end of the lesson. First, she connects homework and text-related work from the previous day to today's lesson. She explains the activity for the day. The students must work in pairs to copy the words of Hamlet's soliloquy and insert 12 interpolated comments or questions directed to Hamlet. During the entire activity, the teacher questions students and challenges them to search and interpret their findings.

- Teacher calls students by name. Students use each other's names when referring to one another. No disrespectful talk is heard during this observation between teacher and students or student-to-student.

- (13:81) T: "If you need to get up or stand up, go ahead and do that."

- Some students begin their explanations by referring to what other students said. "I agree with Lauren because…."

- Students spontaneously help the teacher pass out materials. Many "thank you's" are heard as materials are distributed.

- Students demonstrate perseverance and tolerance toward one another as they work with partners to discern the meaning of Shakespeare's words.

- Random comments that are observed:
  - One girl says, "I don't understand the 'soft' part here? What does he mean?'
  - T: Look at the punctuation.
  - S1 to S2: I don't get that word. Could you look it up? S2 does so. S2: It means disgraced. S2: Oh, so he is like ashamed of her?
  - S: I love that line. Your soul is messed up.
  - S: I think he's just pretending to be crazy.

Record of Evidence

Cluster 2: Safe, Respectful, Supportive, and Challenging Learning Environment

Evidence (cont'd.)

- – S: Why would he do that? It is a soliloquy. Who is he trying to convince? He is the only one there.
- – S: He is really leaning toward crazy here.
- – S: But she is his mom. Everyone gets mad at their mom, but moms deserve respect.
- – One partner group to teacher: Can we use humor? T: Absolutely, if it is in context.
- – T: I have prizes for presenters and they aren't stickers.
- – S: Let me guess. Pencils? Students grin.
- – T: No they are not even pencils. You'll see. She grins.

- With the exception of one set of partners, the work appears to be divided equally between pairs. One writes, one looks up definitions in the Oxford English Dictionary as both discuss. Some share the writing also.

- The teacher circulates, asking and answering questions to assess students' comprehension. Teacher suggests some students rehearse for their presentations when she sees that they are beginning to complete their charts, and they do so. Some rehearse multiple times.

- The teacher asks for volunteers to share their presentations. Four different sets of partners share. They visibly care about their work. One group writes very humorous comments that Hamlet's friend might make to him. T: I'm enjoying your sarcasm. The students' actions and comments show that they feel safe to use humor on their chart, and enjoy having their efforts respected by both their peers and teacher.

- Teacher and students listen with respect and respond positively during presentations. Students applaud politely after each presentation.

- The students put their heads down to vote on the presentation they think best. They seem to conscientiously vote for the partners who worked hardest to find the meaning behind Hamlet's mood.

Record of Evidence

Cluster 2: **Safe, Respectful, Supportive, and Challenging Learning Environment**

Interpretation

- *The "Strive for Excellence" poster seems to be the theme for this classroom and this group of students.*
- *Expectations are clear to almost all students. One boy approaches the teacher for an additional explanation. She willingly gives him the directions again.*
- *There was intermittent student dialogue during partner work.*
- *The teacher's probing responses to students' questions demonstrates respect for their ability to come to their own understanding.*
- *Students struggle, discuss, ask partners for input, and search for textual evidence.*
- *The teacher seems to have a high regard for the students' judgment.*
- *Teacher and students appear comfortable joking with each other.*
- *Multiple rehearsals indicate students care about the quality of their work.*
- *Students show that this is an environment safe for risk-taking by volunteering to present.*
- *Students express appreciation for the efforts of their classmates.*
- *Students clearly value a commitment to excellence, even though they enjoy a humorous presentation from one set of their peers.*

Record of Evidence

Cluster 3:   Classroom Management

Guiding Questions

- *Is the classroom well run and organized?*

- *Are classroom routines and procedures clear and carried out efficiently by both teacher and students with little loss of instructional time?*

- *To what extent do students themselves take an active role in their smooth operation?*

- *Are directions for activities clearly explained so that there is no confusion?*

- *Do students not only understand and comply with standards of conduct, but also play an active part in setting the tone for maintaining those standards?*

- *How does the physical environment support the learning activities?*

Evidence

- Teacher immediately begins class by connecting today's work with the previous day's lesson and homework. She asks questions and listens, building on students' answers while explaining directions for today's lesson. The objective is written on the board and clarified by the teacher.
- Students raise their hands during whole group class discussions and wait to be called upon to share an opinion. Students are attentive as the teacher explains the day's lesson and assignment. The slide show containing soliloquies is clearly visible to all students.
- Desks are arranged in sets of two before the lesson so that the transition to working with partners is very smooth. Assigning students to work with the person sitting next to them, with no movement of students or desks needed, results in no loss of instructional time. Students pass out markers of two different colors while teacher tears and distributes chart papers. Many "thank you's" are heard as the materials are distributed. Students have iPads on their desks when the observation begins. Each pair of students has access to at least one iPad.
- (12:09) Transition from whole group discussion to partner activity takes about 2 minutes. No disruptive behavior is observed.
- Teacher tells students they may stand up if they want to as they work on their chart papers.
- When the teacher asks students to become quiet and listen, they consistently comply without hesitation or complaint.
- When students work as partners, the classroom has an appropriate volume level for nine groups of partners who are having discussions simultaneously. The comments that can be heard in the video confirm that students are on topic during the partner sharing time.

Record of Evidence

Cluster 3:   Classroom Management

Evidence (cont'd.)

- Teacher circulates during the partner activity, using proximity to encourage and assess students' engagement and understanding. There are no paraprofessionals working in the classroom, though videographers are visible.
- No misbehavior is noticed that causes any significant interruption to learning. When enthusiasm gets the better of students, they are quickly brought back to productivity.
- (29:19) T: You have 5 to 7 more minutes to finish.
- (33:20) Teacher notices two students are finished. She tells the students when they finish their work on their chart they may begin rehearsing for the presentations.
- Eight students share presentations while other students listen respectfully and applaud at the end of each presentation.
- T: Fold up your charts so that they don't become a nuisance. The teacher directs the students to fold their chart paper late in the lesson. The folding of the charts cuts down on the noise made by rattling paper during their discussion and gives students a place to write their summative predictions of what they think will happen next.

Interpretation
- *Instructional time is maximized with students engaged bell-to-bell.*
- *Materials are accessible to students.*
- *The material is challenging enough and the time parameters brief enough that there seems to be no time for students to be off task.*
- *There is a safe distance between desks to allow the teacher to move freely when monitoring.*
- *The students are polite as peers give presentations.*
- *The teacher seems to be proactive about procedures that will help the class flow smoothly.*
- *The teacher mentions prizes for presenters but this doesn't happen during this observation. No students complain.*

Record of Evidence

Cluster 4: Student Intellectual Engagement

Guiding Questions

- *To what extent are students intellectually engaged in a classroom of high intellectual energy?*
- *What is the nature of what students are doing?*
- *Are they being challenged to think and make connections through both the instructional activities and the questions explored?*
- *Do the teacher's explanations of content correctly model academic language and invite intellectual work by students?*
- *Are students asked to explain their thinking, to construct logical arguments citing evidence, and to question the thinking of others?*
- *Are the instructional strategies used by the teacher suitable to the discipline, and to what extent do they promote student agency in the learning of challenging content?*

Evidence

- Teacher begins by connecting homework and previous day's lesson to what they will do today. Students hold up fingers to indicate Hamlet's state of mind, basing their opinions on last night's homework video. Some students share their reasoning for selecting the number of fingers they chose to indicate Hamlet's current mental state.
- T: We have mostly between 3 and 4 and a couple of 5s. (1 being sane and 5 indicating crazy). You can put your hands down. Those of you with 3s, why 3?
- S: I don't think he's crazy. He's just putting on a show to make you think he's crazy.
- T: 4s? Why 4?
- S: I think like at first he was in control, now he's out of hand. Losing it. T: Why do you say that? S: Because at times he's very calm and in control, other times he's out of control. T: Do you have a specific example of that? S: Like at the end of scene 2 how out of control, other parts of scene 2, he's calm and mellow.
- T: Someone help him out here. He's saying he is kind of in control here, I just want a little bit of evidence to support that.
- From the teacher's lesson plan: "Students are to work in partners to analyze a Shakespearean soliloquy which is at or above 12th grade level which meets the needs of these students. The soliloquy has a great deal of dark imagery that reflects Hamlet's chaotic mental state."
- There is no evidence that proves the students may or may not make suggestions about the texts that are chosen for the classroom. The assumption is that *Hamlet* is part of the required curriculum to meet the CCSS.
- In pairs, students copy the words of Hamlet's soliloquy "Tis Now the Very Witching Hour" onto chart paper. Each time they reach a punctuation mark within the soliloquy, they are to skip a line. On these blank lines they are to analyze Hamlet's words and then write a response to him as a friend might speak to him. They may

Record of Evidence

Cluster 4: Student Intellectual Engagement

Evidence (cont'd.)

ask him a question about what he means, empathize with him, or use a phrase to calm him. The assignment requires students to write at least 12 responses to Hamlet. They are to change his soliloquy into a dialogue. Students use an iPad version of the Oxford English dictionary to understand the meanings of Hamlet's words.

- Students are asked to explain Hamlet's thinking along with explaining their own thoughts about what they will say to him in return. The partner activity requires that students:
    - Take turns and work cooperatively
    - Cite evidence
    - Use the Oxford English dictionary to clarify the meaning of the words and imagery in the soliloquy
    - Construct logical arguments to defend their interpretations
- The teacher poses higher-level thinking questions that challenge students to form hypotheses during both the full class discussion and the partner discussion. As students work together to discover the meaning behind Hamlet's words, the teacher circulates and monitors by asking such questions as:
    - What do you think is going on in his head?
    - What does he mean by that? Use evidence but tell me in your own words.
    - What would you say to him if he were your best friend?
    - Do Hamlet's words help you predict what will happen in the next acts of this play?
- One set of partners approaches the teacher and asks if their responses can by humorous? T: Yes, if it is in context.
- Teacher engages students by making the partner activity both challenging and fun. She asks students to pretend Horatio is still with Hamlet and create 12 original interruptions that Horatio might say.
- (18:58) T: Guys listen. You don't have to be so serious…hot blood? How about hot chocolate?
- Teacher informs students of time parameters and gives warnings for when the presentations will begin. Four presentations are made involving eight students. Both teacher and students ask questions of the students during their presentations. The presentations evidence the higher-order thinking the students are engaged in when creating their charts. The teacher leads the heads-down voting for the best presentation.
- Teacher brings students back to a large group discussion following the presentations. Students are directed to repeat the finger survey on Hamlet's mental state. More students vote 4 and 5 this time. Teacher asks them to share their reasons.
- The teacher instructs the partners to write a prediction, including textual evidence, on the back of their chart paper explaining what they believe will happen next in the play.

Record of Evidence

Cluster 4: Student Intellectual Engagement

Evidence (cont'd.)

- The students are given less than two minutes to write their predictions and provide evidence to support those opinions.
- The students' written predictions with their evidence for the closing task are not available to the observers.

Interpretation

- *The teacher begins the lesson by connecting previous and future learning to today's work.*
- *The teacher doesn't provide answers, but prods students with questions so that they must seek their own answers.*
- *Students build on each other's ideas.*
- *This statement is found in the teacher's lesson plan: "This activity requires the students to work toward a challenging outcome. Pairs work toward this goal together." The activities throughout the lesson show students carrying out this plan.*
- *This is a creative and challenging activity that calls for student interpretation supported by textual evidence. Student pairs are engaged in productive struggle throughout the classroom. The task requires students to pose higher-order questions to each other.*
- *Students use iPads a number of times to access information from the Oxford English dictionary*
- *The teacher's questions challenge the students to think inside the character's head.*
- *Students modify the learning task to make it more meaningful to them. Teacher supports their request.*
- *The teacher allows students to use current language as long as it supports the text.*
- *Presenters are volunteers from the class. These students are excited about their hypotheses. Voters are discerning about the winner they select.*
- *Students have an opportunity to consolidate their learning with reflection. Many change their previous opinions.*
- *Availability of some of the students' work on the summative assessment would further substantiate the lesson's effectiveness.*

Record of Evidence

Cluster 5:   Successful Learning by All Students
Guiding Questions

- *To what extent does the teacher ensure learning by all students?*

- *Does the teacher monitor student understanding through specifically designed questions or instructional techniques?*

- *To what extent do students monitor their own learning and provide respectful feedback to classmates?*

- *Does the teacher make modifications in presentations or learning activities where necessary, taking into account the degree of student learning?*

- *Has the teacher sought out other resources (including parents) to support students' learning?*

- *In reflection, is the teacher aware of the success of the lesson in reaching students?*

Evidence
- Learning outcomes aligned with CCSS are provided in the lesson plan. Teacher plans for all students to participate in the activities.
- Teacher has heterogeneously paired the students.
- The lesson plan states she will implement the gradual release method. She monitors throughout the lesson, asking questions, listening to students' responses, and providing feedback (often in the form of new questions).
- All pairs have an iPad to use during the full lesson.
- The teacher plans and uses strategies for both formative and summative assessments. The time provided for the summative assessment seems rushed. For a formative assessment, the teacher has students do a finger survey, holding up fingers 1-5 to assess Hamlet's frame of mind. Teacher gives a description for each number.
- Teacher monitors students' understanding during whole group discussions by sharing her thoughts and having students respond. She asks questions, listens to answers, and asks more questions to expand students' learning.
- Students are required to write their 12 interruptions for "Tis Now the Very Witching Time of Night" soliloquy on chart paper. The students are invited to perform the results on their charts, including interpolations, in front of the class after the paired student activity. Teacher allows students to finish writing on their charts while others who have finished rehearse their presentations. During partner work, the teacher circulates to assist and informally assess student comprehension and engagement.
- (16:24) Some students ask what "witching" means. Teacher says aloud to group. "Witching is probably a word you're going to have to look up."

Record of Evidence

Cluster 5:   Successful Learning by All Students

Evidence (cont'd.)

- (17:12) S: Twelve is a lot, but you do need 12? Teacher then says aloud to large group. "Twelve is a lot but you need to look at the punctuation, look for the natural rests in the piece."
- Teacher sometimes models using the students' iPad when monitoring the pair activity.
- Following the pair work and presentations, teacher takes another finger survey.
- T: What do you think about Hamlet's emotional state now?
- S: He's indecisive, his tone, crazy, talking to himself.
- T: There is a change, right?
- S: He starts off talking with negative words and ends with him being more positive. Gets less intense as we read it.
- S (John): Battling against himself, angels and demons on his shoulders. At the beginning of the story angel, pure, after scene two changes more to devil, darker sides of Hamlet.
- T (closure): Last thing I would like you to do with your partner is make a prediction based on the soliloquy and your writings: what is Hamlet going to do in the upcoming scenes? Cite evidence to support that.
- The lesson plan notes that the students will be turning in these responses.
- Teacher comments during interview:
  - Students were referring to their iPad constantly, which is a change from the past.
  - Students used evidence to build on each other's observations and insights.
  - By being paired, the students had to understand text and have conversations.
  - Students were in constant conversations back and forth, sharing their ideas.
  - After doing the exercise, viewing the performances, and returning to large group discussion, students were able to build on ideas and conversations they had in pairs.
- For assisting students with greater needs, the teacher mentions only grouping the students heterogeneously. She assists a student who approaches her by repeating the directions to him individually until he seems to understand. The lesson plan interview and observation do not provide evidence of the teacher informing students she has other methods to assist their efforts if the current strategies fail to help the students comprehend the material.
- The teacher provides no suggestions for ways to improve the lesson in the lesson plan reflection or teacher interview.
- The classroom observation, teacher interview, and documents provided, do not provide evidence for the following:
  - The teacher maintains regular two-way conversations with families or uses the family as a resource.
  - The teacher maintains a coherent record-keeping system.

Record of Evidence

Cluster 5:   Successful Learning by All Students

Interpretation
- *Classroom video (54:30 – 55:45): excellent strategy for most of the students in this class.*
- *The lesson plan mentions two students with 504 plans who may need extended time. The pace of this lesson appears to be challenging for all students and does not reveal any extra time for those students who may need it.*
- *Post group work reflection is provided.*
- *The summative assessment seems rushed.*
- *The teacher seems to meet the needs of most of her students, but may not have met all those of students with greater needs.*

Record of Evidence

Cluster 6:   Professionalism

Guiding Questions

- *To what extent does the teacher engage with the professional community (within the school and beyond) and demonstrate a commitment to ongoing professional learning?*

- *Does the teacher collaborate productively with colleagues and contribute to the life of the school?*

- *Does the teacher engage in professional learning and take a leadership role in the school to promote the welfare of students?*

Evidence

No evidence of Cluster 6 is present in this Instructional Set.

**Looking at Teaching Through
the Lens of the FFT Clusters**

A Study Guide for
Teacher
Learning Communities

Teacher: Glynn
Subject: Math
Grade: 2
Topic: Solving Word Problems

Welcome to the Study Guide for the Glynn Mathematics Instructional Set, a collection of artifacts and videos for an instructional lesson. This Study Guide provides information and instructions on how to examine teaching and learning through the lens of the Framework for Teaching (FFT) Clusters. In order to complete the steps in this Guide, you will need access to the teacher's planning documents, the lesson video, and the teacher commentary video (http://www.danielsongroup.org/study-guides/). Steps 1–5 of this Study Guide focus on examining the Instructional Set and can be done by an individual. Step 6 is a group activity and focuses on sharing results of the analysis and applications of learning.

1

Step 1 - Lesson Overview

Read the background information of the lesson provided below.

This second grade math lesson focuses on Common Core State Standards (CCSS) of operations and algebraic thinking, aspects of rigor, and procedure skill. An additional focus is on students sharing their thinking in a risk-free environment. The students are learning new skills throughout the year while building their knowledge and tool bag of strategies. Students in this lesson work with their teacher in a large group and in table groups to solve various types of single-step word problems.

The teacher guides the students through structured large-group activities. Activities are sequenced to have students begin by reviewing strategies, and then working through problems together using various strategies. The teacher differentiates through student self-assessment and small-group activities designed to meet the needs of each of the small learning groups. The lesson culminates with the teacher introducing a two-step word problem and the students organizing the information in anticipation of the next lesson.

Ms. Glynn explains in the interview how problem solving unfolds over the year from basic to complex. She states that students must read, think about the big picture, determine a strategy, and explain their answer. Ms. Glynn adamantly stresses in both the teacher interview and the instructional plan that her intent is to create a classroom culture where students feel respected enough to explore the use of multiple strategies, are able to use mathematical language, and feel comfortable even if they don't get the right answer.

Step 2 - Preparation and Questions

- *Read the teacher's lesson plan and jot down things you expect to see and what you want to look for in the video of the lesson.*

- *Write down any questions or comments you have about the lesson plan.*

Step 3 – Viewing the Classroom Video

- *View the complete video, noting those things you expected to see based on the lesson plan. Also note what was missing based on your expectations from the lesson plan. Jot down significant behaviors by the teacher and students pertinent to the FFT Clusters.*

4

Step 4 – Selected Highlights of the Lesson Video

Read the highlights of the lesson provided below. Note those matching your highlights of the lesson. For each set of statements, determine the FFT Cluster that is best related to the behaviors presented.

Ms. Glynn, demonstrates the power of creating a culture of learning in which students are confident enough to self-assess. The teacher shows a determination that the students will master the lesson in an environment where they feel comfortable to share, explore many strategies, and persevere. She states in the reflection, "Students can take a risk and not worry if their answer is wrong."

A. *Calling the students by name (referring to them as "my friends") and modeling respectful interactions (such as thanking students for their responses and sharing their ideas) demonstrate genuine caring. Students are respectful when they raise their hands to volunteer answers and do not talk over each other. (Cluster ___)*

B. *The teacher leads the students in a review of what perseverance means and how it applies to their lesson of problem solving. The students persevere throughout the lesson, choosing strategies and solving problems. (Cluster ___)*

C. *The classroom operates smoothly and efficiently and there is no loss of instructional time. Several procedures and routines are in place to which both the teacher and students react automatically (e.g., 3, 2, 1 strategy to bring attention to the teacher, thumbs up or pencil down, students responding to the rain stick, and students moving to new groups quickly). (Cluster ___)*

D. *The teacher instructs students to choose the strategies that will work best for them in solving the problems, thereby*

---

challenging the students to do the thinking. The strategies are designed so that students with a more advanced level of skill may choose strategies that allow them to eliminate some steps. (Cluster ___)

E. *The teacher models the problem-solving process as she works through the first problem with the students on the SmartBoard. She ask students to explain their thinking as she moves through the problem ("Why did you choose that? Where did you go from there? Can you tell me why you decided to put the blank here?") (Cluster ___)*

F. *The teacher gives the students the opportunity to self-assess their own learning and self-select one of three groups, based on how confident they are in solving word problems. The teacher asks the students if they should move to a group of others they would like to be with, or to one where they will move forward in their learning. (Cluster ___)*

Step 5 – Viewing the Teacher Commentary

Watch the video of the teacher's commentary about the lesson and jot down any questions or comments you have about the commentary. Read the highlights below and identify the related FFT Cluster.

A. The teacher talks about the skills and prior knowledge the students have developed to solve word problems. She explains that students work on problem solving all year and the work becomes increasingly difficult. (Cluster ___)

B. Besides focusing on solving one-step word problems, the teacher also emphasizes Core Action 3, stressing the importance of an environment of trust and risk-taking in order to establish a culture where students explain their thinking during respectful discussions. (Cluster ___)

C. The teacher explains that in the past, the focus was on getting the answer. Under the CCSS, students now need to read to determine what information is important, and decide how to use an efficient strategy to solve the problem. The focus is on the process and on students being able to explain their thinking. (Cluster ___)

D. The teacher explains at the end of the commentary that the students did get the math, and the different options in their tool bags differentiated the lesson for them. She believes that she has built an environment where the students understand and respect that it's all right to use different strategies and solve problems in different ways. (Cluster ___)

Step 6 – Questions, Applications, and Discussion

The purpose of this step is to prompt your analysis and reflection of the Instructional Set and to have you think about applications to your own practice.

1. Teaching and Learning Related to the FFT Clusters

The purpose of the activity is to increase your understanding of the relationship between the highlights of the Instructional Set and the FFT Clusters. Your identification of an FFT Cluster for each of the highlights is compared to the Cluster identified by the master coders. The Answer Key is located at the end of the activities. You have options on how to complete the comparison. Determine what might work best for your group's learning. Options include, but are not limited to the following.

- Look at the first set of highlights. Take a poll of what each group member identified as the related FFT Cluster. If all members said the same FFT Cluster, have one or two

FFT Clusters Study Guide: Set 4 (Math 2)

members say why. Compare the group's response to the answer sheet. Repeat for the remainder of the highlights.

OR

- Have each member take one or two highlights. State the correct answer for each one, and a reason why the highlight demonstrates that FFT Cluster. The member will facilitate a discussion if others had different responses, with the goal of having all understand the justification of the correct answer.

OR

- Have members check their own responses to all the highlights. If there are any incorrect answers, then the member selects one highlight and leads a discussion with the group to learn why others think the highlight matches the correct FFT Cluster.

OR

- Determine your own process to check and discuss the match between highlights and the FFT Clusters.

2. **Analysis and Reflection of the Instructional Set**

The purpose of this activity is for you to analyze and reflect on what you saw and heard in the artifacts and videos, to share your analysis with your peers, and to discuss some of the questions or comments you noted. Review the notes, comments, and questions you recorded when you examined the Instructional Set.

- Identify a key teaching and learning attribute demonstrated in the Instructional Set that was effective and state why you think it worked well.

- Identify a different attribute and provide ideas about how it could be enhanced or improved.

- Share your statements with your group and have your peers react to and build upon your analysis and ideas.

Sample statements:

One of the strengths noticed in the lesson was the opportunity for students to self-assess their own learning and then self-select one of three groups based on how confident they are in solving word problems. I would want to know, in what ways the teacher thought the lesson went as planned. Because the students were self-assessing, I wonder how the teacher knew they had increased their capabilities. I think the student-led small groups were successful because the students appeared to have previously learned the skills to work in groups. The teacher worked with students who she determined needed the most help. I would ask the teacher if a more formal assessment of students' work would show her the progress of the other two groups.

Additional ideas for statements:

- Degree to which students take pride in their work and demonstrate a commitment to mastering challenging content

- Extent to which the instructional strategies used by the teacher are appropriate for the discipline

- Extent to which students monitor their own learning and provide feedback to others

- Extent to which the teacher provides wait time to allow students time to think and construct an answer

3. **Notice, Learn, and Apply**

The purpose of this activity is for you to reflect on what you learned from your analysis of the Instructional Set and to determine how you will apply it to your teaching.

- Complete the statements:
  "I noticed _____."
  (Insert one thing you noticed about the teacher or students.)

  "And I learned _____."
  (State what you learned related to what you noticed.)

  "I will apply what I learned by _____."
  (Provide example of how you will use what you learned in your own context.)

- Share your statements with your group. Have others react and add how they might apply what you noticed to their own teaching context.

Sample statement:

- I noticed the teacher introduced the two-step word problem at the end of the lesson using enthusiastic language, generating excitement among the students for what comes next.

- I learned that if the teacher is excited about learning, the students will be eager to move forward.

- I will apply what I learned as I share with students and colleagues my enthusiasm for the learning (creating and practicing specific language), and I will create lessons that convey the message there is always new learning to come.

Study Guide for Teachers Answer Key

Highlights from the Lesson Video (Step 4)

A. Calling the students by name (referring to them as "my friends") and modeling respectful interactions (such as thanking students for their responses and sharing their ideas) demonstrate genuine caring. Students are respectful of each when they raise their hands to volunteer answers and do not talk over each other. (Cluster 2 Safe, Respectful, Supportive and Challenging Learning Environment)

B. The teacher leads the students in a review of what perseverance means and how it applies to their lesson of problem solving. The students persevere throughout the lesson, choosing strategies and solving problems. (Cluster 2 Safe, Respectful, Supportive and Challenging Learning Environment)

C. The classroom operates smoothly and efficiently and there is no loss of instructional time. Several procedures and routines are in place to which both the teacher and students react automatically (e.g., 3, 2, 1 strategy to bring attention to the teacher, thumbs up or pencil down, students responding to the rain stick, and students moving to new groups quickly). (Cluster 3 Classroom Management)

D. The teacher instructs students to choose the strategies that will work best for them in solving the problems, thereby challenging the students to do the thinking. The strategies are designed so that students with a more advanced level of skill may choose strategies that allow them to eliminate some steps. (Cluster 4 Student Intellectual Engagement)

E. The teacher models the problem-solving process as she works through the first problem with the students on the SmartBoard. She ask students to explain their thinking as she moves through the problem ("Why did you choose that? Where did you go from there? Can you tell me why you decided to put the blank here?") (Cluster 4 Student Intellectual Engagement)

F. The teacher gives the students the opportunity to self-assess their own learning and self-select one of three groups, based on how confident they are in solving word problems. The teacher asks the students if they should move to a group of others they would like to be with, or to one where they will move forward in their learning. (Cluster 5 Successful Learning by all students)

Study Guide for Teachers Answer Key

Highlights from the Teacher Commentary (Step 5)

A. The teacher talks about the skills and prior knowledge the students have developed to solve word problems. She explains that students work on problem solving all year and the work becomes increasingly difficult. (Cluster 1 Clarity of Instructional Purpose and Accuracy of Content)

B. Besides focusing on solving one-step word problems, the teacher also emphasizes Core Action 3, stressing the importance of an environment of trust and risk-taking in order to establish a culture where students explain their thinking during respectful discussions. (Cluster 1 Clarity of Instructional Purpose and Accuracy of Content)

C. The teacher explains that in the past, the focus was on getting to the answer. Under the CCSS, students now need to read to determine what information is important, and decide how to use an efficient strategy to solve the problem. The focus is on the process and on students being able to explain their thinking. (Cluster 1 Clarity of Instructional Purpose and Accuracy of Content)

D. The teacher explains at the end of the commentary that the students did get the math, and the different options in their tool bags differentiated the lesson for them. She believes that she has built an environment where the students understand and respect that it's all right to use different strategies and solve problems in different ways. (Cluster 5 Successful Learning by All Students

**Looking at Teaching Through
the Lens of the FFT Clusters**

A Study Guide for
Instructional Coach
Learning Communities

Teacher: Glynn
Subject: Math
Grade: 2
Topic: Solving Word Problems

Welcome to the Study Guide for the Glynn Mathematics Instructional Set, a collection of artifacts and videos for an instructional lesson. This Study Guide provides information and instructions on how to examine teaching and learning through the lens of the Framework for Teaching (FFT) Clusters. In order to complete the steps in this Guide, you will need access to the teacher's planning documents, the lesson video, and the teacher commentary video (http://www.danielsongroup.org/study-guides/). Steps 1–5 of this Study Guide focus on examining the Instructional Set and can be done by an individual. Step 6 is a group activity and focuses on sharing results of the analysis and applications of learning.

 ### Step 1 - Lesson Overview

Read the background information of the lesson provided below.

This second grade math lesson focuses on Common Core State Standards (CCSS) of operations and algebraic thinking, aspects of rigor, and procedure skill. An additional focus is on students sharing their thinking in a risk-free environment. The students are learning new skills throughout the year while building their knowledge and tool bag of strategies. Students in this lesson work with their teacher in a large group and in table groups to solve various types of single-step word problems.

The teacher guides the students through structured large-group activities. Activities are sequenced to have students begin by reviewing strategies, and then working through problems together using various strategies. The teacher differentiates through student self-assessment and small-group activities designed to meet the needs of each of the small learning groups. The lesson culminates with the teacher introducing a two-step word problem and the students organizing the information in anticipation of the next lesson.

Ms. Glynn explains in the interview how problem solving unfolds over the year from basic to complex. She states that students must read, think about the big picture, determine a strategy, and explain their answer. Ms. Glynn adamantly stresses in both the teacher interview and the instructional plan that her intent is to create a classroom culture where students feel respected enough to explore the use of multiple strategies, are able to use mathematical language, and feel comfortable even if they don't get the right answer.

Step 2 - Preparation and Questions

- *Read the teacher's lesson plan and jot down things you expect to see and what you want to look for in the video of the lesson.*

- *Write down any questions or comments you have about the lesson plan.*

Step 3 – Viewing the Classroom Video

- *View the complete video, noting those things you expected to see based on the lesson plan. Also note what was missing based on your expectations from the lesson plan. Jot down significant behaviors by the teacher and students pertinent to the FFT Clusters.*

Step 4 – Selected Highlights of the Lesson Video

Read the highlights of the lesson provided below. Note those matching your highlights of the lesson. For each set of statements, determine the FFT Cluster that is best related to the behaviors presented.

Ms. Glynn, demonstrates the power of creating a culture of learning in which students are confident enough to self-assess. The teacher shows a determination that the students will master the lesson in an environment where they feel comfortable to share, explore many strategies, and persevere. She states in the reflection, "Students can take a risk and not worry if their answer is wrong."

> A. *Calling the students by name (referring to them as "my friends") and modeling respectful interactions (such as thanking students for their responses and sharing their ideas) demonstrate genuine caring. Students are respectful when they raise their hands to volunteer answers and do not talk over each other. (Cluster ____)*
>
> B. *The teacher leads the students in a review of what perseverance means and how it applies to their lesson of problem solving. The students persevere throughout the lesson, choosing strategies and solving problems. (Cluster ____)*
>
> C. *The classroom operates smoothly and efficiently and there is no loss of instructional time. Several procedures and routines are in place to which both the teacher and students react automatically (e.g., 3, 2, 1 strategy to bring attention to the teacher, thumbs up or pencil down, students responding to the rain stick, and students moving to new groups quickly). (Cluster ____)*
>
> D. *The teacher instructs students to choose the strategies that will work best for them in solving the problems, thereby challenging the students to do the thinking. The strategies*

are designed so that students with a more advanced level of skill may choose strategies that allow them to eliminate some steps. (Cluster ___)

E. The teacher models the problem-solving process as she works through the first problem with the students on the SmartBoard. She ask students to explain their thinking as she moves through the problem ("Why did you choose that? Where did you go from there? Can you tell me why you decided to put the blank here?") (Cluster ___)

F. The teacher gives the students the opportunity to self-assess their own learning and self-select one of three groups, based on how confident they are in solving word problems. The teacher asks the students if they should move to a group of others they would like to be with, or to one where they will move forward in their learning. (Cluster ___)

Step 5 – Viewing the Teacher Commentary

Watch the video of the teacher's commentary about the lesson and jot down any questions or comments you have about the commentary. Read the highlights below and identify the related FFT Cluster.

A. The teacher talks about the skills and prior knowledge the students have developed to solve word problems. She explains that students work on problem solving all year and the work becomes increasingly difficult. (Cluster ___)

B. Besides focusing on solving one-step word problems, the teacher also emphasizes Core Action 3, stressing the importance of an environment of trust and risk-taking in order to establish a culture where students explain their thinking during respectful discussions. (Cluster ___)

C. The teacher explains that in the past, the focus was on getting the answer. Under the CCSS, students now need to read to determine what information is important, and decide how to use an efficient strategy to solve the problem. The focus is on the process and on students being able to explain their thinking. (Cluster ____)

D. The teacher explains at the end of the commentary that the students did get the math, and the different options in their tool bags differentiated the lesson for them. She believes that she has built an environment where the students understand and respect that it's all right to use different strategies and solve problems in different ways. (Cluster ___)

Step 6 – Questions, Applications, and Discussion

The purpose of this step is to prompt your analysis and reflection of the Instructional Set and to have you think about applications to your own practice.

1. **Teaching and Learning Related to the FFT Clusters**

The purpose of the activity is to increase your understanding of the relationship between the highlights of the Instructional Set and the FFT Clusters. Your identification of an FFT Cluster for each of the highlights is compared to the Cluster identified by the master coders. The Answer Key is located at the end of the activities. You have options on how to complete the comparison. Determine what might work best for your group's learning. Options include, but are not limited to the following.

- Look at the first set of highlights. Take a poll of what each group member identified as the related FFT Cluster. If all members said the same FFT Cluster, then have one or two members say why. Compare the group's response to the answer sheet. Repeat for the remainder of the sets of highlights.

OR

- Have each member take one or two sets of highlights and be the discussant for them. The discussant will state the correct answer and state a reason why the statements in the set demonstrate the FFT Cluster. The discussant will facilitate a discussion if members had different responses with the goal of all understanding the justification of the correct answer.

OR

- Have members check their own responses to all the sets of highlights. If there are any incorrect answers, then the member selects one set and leads a discussion with the group to learn why others think the highlights match the correct FFT Cluster.

OR

- Determine your own process to check and discuss the match between highlights and the FFT Clusters.

2. **Analysis and Reflection of the Instructional Set**

The purpose of this activity is for you to analyze and reflect on what you saw and heard in the artifacts and videos and to discuss some of the questions or comments you noted. One element of a professional conversation is asking questions to ascertain more information about a teacher's thinking and the behaviors of both students and teacher. This activity allows you and your peers to practice preparing such questions. Your peers can comment on whether your questions are appropriate and will obtain useful information without making the featured teacher feel uneasy or criticized.

The second part of this activity focuses on helping teachers move their practice forward. Please note that having you prepare for and model an entire conversation about the lesson with the featured teacher is not the purpose of this activity as written. Your group can modify or replace the activity to meet your group's needs

- Review the notes, comments, and questions you recorded when you examined the Instructional Set. Pretend you have the opportunity to ask the teacher some questions to get additional information about the strategies used or decisions made for this Instructional Set.

- Share with your group just the questions you would use with the teacher to elicit additional information. Have your peers comment about your questions and add other questions they had about the same event.

- Share with others in your group what you would do to prompt the teacher's thinking and actions to enhance his/her practice. Take turns sharing and discussing the prompts.

Sample A, Part I:

I noticed that during the small group discussion, one of the students, Marcos, does not share a strategy. His tablemate respectfully invites him to add his thoughts. Because Marcos was able to share a strategy, I wonder what he was thinking during the discussion? What do you think? What do you think the other students at the table might have been thinking?

Sample A, Part II:

What expectations did you have for students to share during small group discussion? How did the students know those expectations? How might other groups of students learn from this respectful conversation?

Sample B, Part I:

You used the SmartBoard extensively to organize and record strategies and to walk students through the two-step process. Students both heard and saw the lesson. What did you notice about the effectiveness of using visual and auditory strategies? When thinking about other learning styles (e.g., kinesthetic), how might providing appropriate activities for those learners create opportunities for deeper thinking and understanding?

Sample B, Part II:

If you had the opportunity to teach this lesson again, what might be some ways you could address all learning styles? Given what you know about your students and their learning styles, what might you need to support your learning? What might be some things you will pay attention to in yourself as you stretch your thinking to include all learner preferences?

3. **Notice, Learn, and Apply**

The purpose of this activity is for you to reflect on what you learned from your analysis of the Instructional Set and to determine how you will apply it to your teaching.

- Complete the statements:
  "I noticed _____."
  (Insert one thing you noticed about the teacher or students.)

"And I learned _____."
(State what you learned related to what you noticed.)

"I will apply what I learned by _____."
(Provide example of how you will use what you learned in your own context.)

- Share your statements with your group. Have others react and add how they might apply what you noticed to their own coaching context.

Sample statements:

- I noticed that the teacher encourages both visual and auditory learners. This teacher behavior also serves as a model for students when they are engaged in small group discussion and in giving feedback to their peers.

- I learned that all student learning style preferences need to be honored so all students have the best opportunity to learn.

- I will apply what I learned when creating lessons, modeling for students, and having conversations. Specifically, when working with colleagues, I will pay attention to the way I create activities and engage in conversations.

Study Guide for Instructional Coaches Answer Key

Highlights from the Lesson Video (Step 4)

A. Calling the students by name (referring to them as "my friends") and modeling respectful interactions (such as thanking students for their responses and sharing their ideas) demonstrate genuine caring. Students are respectful of each when they raise their hands to volunteer answers and do not talk over each other. (Cluster 2 Safe, Respectful, Supportive and Challenging Learning Environment)

B. The teacher leads the students in a review of what perseverance means and how it applies to their lesson of problem solving. The students persevere throughout the lesson, choosing strategies and solving problems. (Cluster 2 Safe, Respectful, Supportive and Challenging Learning Environment)

C. The classroom operates smoothly and efficiently and there is no loss of instructional time. Several procedures and routines are in place to which both the teacher and students react automatically (e.g., 3, 2, 1 strategy to bring attention to the teacher, thumbs up or pencil down, students responding to the rain stick, and students moving to new groups quickly). (Cluster 3 Classroom Management)

D. The teacher instructs students to choose the strategies that will work best for them in solving the problems, thereby challenging the students to do the thinking. The strategies are designed so that students with a more advanced level of skill may choose strategies that allow them to eliminate some steps. (Cluster 4 Student Intellectual Engagement)

E. The teacher models the problem-solving process as she works through the first problem with the students on the SmartBoard. She ask students to explain their thinking as she moves through the problem ("Why did you choose that? Where did you go from there? Can you tell me why you decided to put the blank here?") (Cluster 4 Student Intellectual Engagement)

F. The teacher gives the students the opportunity to self-assess their own learning and self-select one of three groups, based on how confident they are in solving word problems. The teacher asks the students if they should move to a group of others they would like to be with, or to one where they will move forward in their learning. (Cluster 5 Successful Learning by all students)

Study Guide for Instructional Coaches Answer Key

Highlights from the Teacher Commentary (Step 5)

A. The teacher talks about the skills and prior knowledge the students have developed to solve word problems. She explains that students work on problem solving all year and the work becomes increasingly difficult. (Cluster 1 Clarity of Instructional Purpose and Accuracy of Content)

B. Besides focusing on solving one-step word problems, the teacher also emphasizes Core Action 3, stressing the importance of an environment of trust and risk-taking in order to establish a culture where students explain their thinking during respectful discussions. (Cluster 1 Clarity of Instructional Purpose and Accuracy of Content)

C. The teacher explains that in the past, the focus was on getting to the answer. Under the CCSS, students now need to read to determine what information is important, and decide how to use an efficient strategy to solve the problem. The focus is on the process and on students being able to explain their thinking. (Cluster 1 Clarity of Instructional Purpose and Accuracy of Content)

D. The teacher explains at the end of the commentary that the students did get the math, and the different options in their tool bags differentiated the lesson for them. She believes that she has built an environment where the students understand and respect that it's all right to use different strategies and solve problems in different ways. (Cluster 5 Successful Learning by All Students

Record of Evidence

This Record of Evidence (ROE) contains key evidence aligned to the FFT Clusters. Interpretive statements about the evidence are also provided. The ROE was created by two master coders who recorded evidence and interpretation statements independently, reviewed each others' work, and arrived at a final composite version based on their professional conversations. This version was reviewed by a leader of the master coders. The ROE is included in this Study Guide so users can see what master coders identified as key evidence, and their interpretation of that evidence through the lens of the FFT Clusters. It is provided as an example of one type of analysis of an Instructional Set. The ROEs were created for professional development rather than evaluative purposes. Users are cautioned about using them for teacher evaluation.

Rubric:	Generic
Grade:	2
Subject:	Math
Topic:	Solving Word Problems
Teacher description:	Female, white
Class description:	The class comprises 25 second grade students. 14 students (56%) receive free lunch. 7 (28%) students are English Language Learners (2 at an emerging level, 4 at a developing level and 1 at an expanding level). There are 2 students with Individual Education Plans, one of which is academic and the student receives literacy and math instruction outside the general education classroom; the other student has a speech IEP but it does not affect his performance. According to the fall Curriculum Based Measurement in math concepts and applications, 18 (72%) are Tier One, 2 (8%) are Tier Two, and 5 (20%) are Tier Three
Artifacts:	• Lesson plan • Teacher commentary
Length of video:	35:55

Record of Evidence

Cluster 1: Clarity of Instructional Purpose and Accuracy of Content
Guiding Questions

- *To what extent does the teacher demonstrate depth of important content knowledge and conduct the class with a clear and ambitious purpose, reflective of the standards for the discipline and appropriate to the students' levels of knowledge and skill?*

- *To what degree are the elements of a lesson (the sequence of topics, instructional strategies, and materials and resources) well designed and executed, and aligned with the purpose of the lesson?*

- *To what extent are they designed to engage students in high-level learning in the discipline?*

Evidence

Instructional Plan

- The teacher correlates this lesson to the Common Core math standards for grade 2: 2.OA.A.1 Operations and Algebraic Thinking: Use addition and subtraction within 100 to solve one- and two-step word problems involving situations of adding to, taking from, putting together, taking apart, and comparing with unknowns in all positions by using drawings and equations with a symbol for the unknown number to represent the problem.
- The teacher writes that the focus for this lesson will be on the various types of single-step word problems (putting together, start unknown, and change unknown).
  1. *Conceptual Understanding*: The students will be able to determine the type of word problem that is being solved (putting together, start unknown, or change unknown) based on the information that is provided in each problem.
  2. *Procedural Skill*: The students will identify and organize the information given in the problem, and determine strategies that can be used to solve it.
  3. *Fluency and Application*: Students can use their knowledge of addition/subtraction facts to solve word problems; students will be able to apply various strategies to solve and check their thinking.
- The teacher's plans indicate she will use the following materials: SmartBoard lesson notebook, white board slates, dry erase markers, ELMO, pencils, packet of word problems, bags with tools for optional student use (base 10 blocks, number lines, counters, and ten frames).
- The teacher has a detailed lesson plan that outlines the following steps:
  Anticipatory Set
    – Introduce the learning target for the lesson ("I can use different strategies to persevere in solving word problems.") Review what it means to persevere.
    – Ask students to brainstorm strategies at their tables that we have used in solving word problems from previous lessons.

Record of Evidence

Cluster 1:   Clarity of Instructional Purpose and Accuracy of Content

Evidence (cont'd.)

- Share team discussions with whole class as teacher collects ideas in circle map (Thinking Map).

Lesson

- Review procedures for solving word problems (organize information, use a strategy to solve, use a second strategy to check work, be ready to explain your thinking).
- Display a word problem (putting together) on the board, choral reading of the problem, students solve it on slates using the optional tool bags as they desire.
- Volunteers show slate under the ELMO and describe a strategy that they used and their thinking as they solved the problem.
- Display a new word problem (change unknown) on the board, choral read the problem, students solve it on slates using the optional tool bags as they desire.
- Students share their strategies and thinking at their tables.
- Teacher displays a self-assessment target on the board. Students determine where they fall on the target to determine the learning group that meets their needs.
- Group 1: Feel they are meeting the target and can help a partner, or are mostly meeting the target but may need help from a partner. This group will be given a packet containing a variety of word problems. They will have their slates and tool bags as optional resources, and will find a spot on the floor around the room where they can work. Students will read the problem together, solve individually, and then share their strategies. If the students come up with different answers, they will review their work together to try to find the error.
- Group 2: Feels they will best meet their learning needs by working in a small group with the teacher. Students have the option of joining an independent group as they feel comfortable. This group will join the teacher at the front of the room to continue solving word problems. The problems will be displayed on the board and read together. Students will also have the word problems in their packets. After the problems are read, students will organize the information and use two strategies to solve and check their work. Students will share their strategies and thinking.

Teacher Commentary

- The teacher explains how problem solving unfolds over the year, from basic to more complex. Teacher has worked to create an environment where students can explain their thinking and feel comfortable even if they don't get the right answer. In the past, students focused on key words in order to determine how to solve the problem. Now, with Common Core, there is no consistent pattern, and key words don't give away the procedure. Students must read, think about the big picture,

Record of Evidence

Cluster 1: Clarity of Instructional Purpose and Accuracy of Content

Evidence (cont'd.)

and determine a strategy. Now the focus is on problem solving and being able to explain their answer. This is a strategy that is worked on throughout the year. Students can take a risk, and not worry if their answer is wrong.

- Reflection: The students did get the math of the lesson. Some students who are still at the beginning stages of place value can use manipulatives to help them solve their problems. More advanced students use the expanded form and don't need the manipulative so much. Others just use the numbers themselves. Options make it accessible for all. Differentiated by using different tools from their tool bags. Some students who are basic are still drawing pictures and counting up. Other do counting by tens. We work on having that respect for one another, understanding that students do it in different ways. It took time for me to build that environment where students could take risks and explain their answers.

Video

- The teacher's instructions to the students are clear. She monitors for accuracy, asking, for example, to point to where their name goes on the paper.
- The teacher goes over the learning target with the students and has them read it together. "I can persevere in solving word problems using many strategies." The class discusses the meaning of persevere.
- T: We're going to turn to the first word problem in our packet. The teacher works through the problem with the students and models the steps on the white board:
  1. Organize
  2. Pick a Strategy
  3. Pick Another Strategy
  4. Solve
- T: Take out your math tool bag and all of those helpful things you might choose to use with your strategies.
- The teacher spends most of the period working through a word problem with the students, reinforcing the procedures, steps, strategies, and thinking required. She models as the students do the thinking.
- At the end of the period, they look ahead at a new type of word problem to show the students where they are going next.

Record of Evidence

Cluster 1:   Clarity of Instructional Purpose and Accuracy of Content

Interpretation

- *The teacher's lesson plan reflects a depth of important content knowledge, both conceptual and procedural. The use of differing strategies allows students to choose methods appropriate to their level of development. The teacher sequences the lesson so that students begin by reviewing strategies for solving word problems, and then work through a problem together using various strategies.*

- *The lesson includes time for student self-assessment and differentiation of instruction.*

- *Work continues on establishing a culture of perseverance and student thinking.*

- *The teacher identifies the learning target in student-friendly language.*

- *The lesson has a clear structure.*

Record of Evidence

Cluster 2:   Safe, Respectful, Supportive, and Challenging Learning Environment

Guiding Questions

- *To what extent do the interactions between teacher and students, and among students, demonstrate genuine caring and a safe, respectful, supportive, and also challenging learning environment?*

- *Do teachers convey high expectations for student learning and encourage hard work and perseverance? Is the environment safe for risk taking?*

- *Do students take pride in their work and demonstrate a commitment to mastering challenging content?*

Evidence

- The teacher discusses the meaning of persevere with the students and they share their ideas.
- T: We need to remember perseverance, because sometimes, these word problems can be hard!
- At the beginning of the lesson, students share strategies they know with their teammates. Students are voluntarily sharing ideas, some new (e.g., "my uncle says…," "my mom showed me…").
- Student interaction is respectful.
- Many hands are raised; students are anxious to share their ideas with the class.
- T: This is a lot of strategies!
- Teacher discusses the meaning of efficient and a way to solve a math problem. T: It has to be good work, a strategy that is helpful in solving the problem. It has to lead to the solution.
- Teacher tells students to pick two strategies to solve the problem; they can use anything in their tool bags to help them solve the problem.
- The steps involve coming up with two strategies, one to solve, and one to check for accuracy.
- T: This time you are going to come up with your strategies and share with your table.
- Teacher calls students "friends" on at least 3 occasions.
- T (when students self-assess their understanding against the learning target to determine their next group): All of us are going to be working to get better from where we are. We can always, always improve.

Record of Evidence

Cluster 2:   Safe, Respectful, Supportive, and Challenging Learning Environment

Evidence (cont'd.)

- Teacher asks if it is more important to be with someone they wanted to work with or in a place that will meet their needs. Student tells classmates to pick the spot that would help them get better.

Interpretation

- *The teacher has worked hard to create a safe, respectful learning environment in which she holds high expectations for student achievement and encourages perseverance and risk taking. Students take pride in their work, and their perseverance shows a commitment to mastering this content.*

- *Students volunteer to share their thinking and are respectful of other student's ideas.*

- *The lesson allows for student choice in the tools and strategies they use to solve the problems posed by the teacher.*

- *The teacher models the respectful relationships that she wants students to have with each other.*

Record of Evidence

Cluster 3:   Classroom Management
Guiding Questions

- *Is the classroom well run and organized?*

- *Are classroom routines and procedures clear and carried out efficiently by both teacher and students with little loss of instructional time?*

- *To what extent do students themselves take an active role in their smooth operation?*

- *Are directions for activities clearly explained so that there is no confusion?*

- *Do students not only understand and comply with standards of conduct, but also play an active part in setting the tone for maintaining those standards?*

- *How does the physical environment support the learning activities?*

Evidence
- Students raise their hands to speak.
- Students are seated at desks facing one another, in groups of four to five students. There is plenty of room for the teacher to move about the groups. There is a colorful carpet in the room with math symbols (numbers, etc.).
- Teacher uses the strategy 3, 2, 1 to bring attention back to her.
- Student behavior throughout the lesson is entirely appropriate. Students stay in their seats the entire period and all are observed working throughout the lesson.
- As students work in a small group, one student, Marcos, had not shared a strategy with the group. A tablemate invites him to add his thoughts on strategies that could be used to solve word problems.
- T: Give me up a thumbs up when you are ready.
- T: Set your pencil down and show me you are ready.
- The teacher has students put all their materials away as they transition to a new activity. The procedure unfolds quickly. She is going to divide them into two self-selected groups.
- T: Please push in your chairs and go to where you belong. Students move quickly to their new groups.
- T: Nice job remembering what this sound means. When you get to your desk, move all the way to the last word problem. We're not going to solve it, just read.
- The teacher uses the white board extensively, projecting the graphic organizer that shows the steps involved in solving the problem. This graphic is visible throughout the lesson, and the teacher is able to fill in information on the organizer as the students work.

Record of Evidence

Cluster 3: Classroom Management

Interpretation

- *The classroom functions smoothly. Little time is wasted on non-instructional tasks.*

- *Students remain productively engaged throughout the lesson.*

- *Student behavior is entirely appropriate.*

- *The physical arrangement of the room supports group discussion as well as large-group work.*

Record of Evidence

Cluster 4: Student Intellectual Engagement

Guiding Questions

- *To what extent are students intellectually engaged in a classroom of high intellectual energy?*

- *What is the nature of what students are doing?*

- *Are they being challenged to think and make connections through both the instructional activities and the questions explored?*

- *Do the teacher's explanations of content correctly model academic language and invite intellectual work by students?*

- *Are students asked to explain their thinking, to construct logical arguments citing evidence, and to question the thinking of others?*

- *Are the instructional strategies used by the teacher suitable to the discipline, and to what extent do they promote student agency in the learning of challenging content?*

Evidence

- The teacher uses mathematical language: place value, ten blocks, brace map, hundreds chart, open number lines, fact families, ten frame, expanded form.
- The teacher reviews numerous strategies for mathematical problem solving with the students at the beginning of class. The students brainstorm in groups, then share with the whole class.
- The teacher reminds the class that students might use different strategies to solve a problem.
- The teacher works through the first problem with the students. She models as they work. First, she has them circle the important information in the word problem. Students share what they chose as important information. Students continue to share and teacher repeats. Next, teacher moves to the second step, asking students what strategies they might use. Next, teacher models with the class: Organize. She emphasizes "label."
- T: Why did you choose that?
- T: Who would like to explain how they organized their information? Student explains. Teacher asks questions during the explanation, moving the argument forward.
- T: Where did you go from there? Why did you write that word? What else did you do? Can you tell me why you decided to put the blank here?
- She shares that their next target will be to use their strategies to solve two-step problems. Student suggests that they will have to add the 20 and 15 and then see how much is left. Teacher explains to students that they will have to do adding and subtracting in that problem to come to the answer.

Record of Evidence

Cluster 4: Student Intellectual Engagement

Interpretation

- *This classroom is cognitively busy, with students identifying important details in a word problem, selecting one or more strategies to solve it, and explaining their choices to the teacher and to other students.*

- *The teacher has provided the students with an array of strategies they may use, ranging from the most concrete to more abstract reasoning models. Students at a more advanced skill level choose strategies that are "more efficient," in that they can eliminate some of the concrete steps.*

- *Teacher scaffolds the learning by introducing two-step problems.*

Record of Evidence

Cluster 5: Successful Learning by All Students
Guiding Questions

- *To what extent does the teacher ensure learning by all students?*

- *Does the teacher monitor student understanding through specifically designed questions or instructional techniques?*

- *To what extent do students monitor their own learning and provide respectful feedback to classmates?*

- *Does the teacher make modifications in presentations or learning activities where necessary, taking into account the degree of student learning?*

- *Has the teacher sought out other resources (including parents) to support students' learning?*

- *In reflection, is the teacher aware of the success of the lesson in reaching students?*

Evidence
- The teacher emphasizes that students can use different strategies to solve problems. She explains in the teacher interview that students will self-select strategies based on their development; basic students will use strategies different from more advanced students.
- T: Did anyone else use the brace map?
- T: You can use anything else in your bag that will help you figure out the information.
- T: I see some of you are using the number line, some using the base ten, etc. Teacher is reinforcing that students are using different strategies.
- T: Is there a different strategy that you might have used? Either way, just make sure that when it comes time to share, you can explain it.
- Teacher monitors thinking by asking students to explain their thinking.
- T: Why did you choose that"
- T: Who would like to explain how they organized their information? Student explains. Teacher asks questions during the explanation, moving the argument forward.
- T: Where did you go from there? Why did you write that word? What else did you do? Can you tell me why you decided to put the blank here?
- Students monitor their own learning and self-select one of two groups to move to, based on how confident they are in solving their word problems.

Closing/Reflection:
- Students will return to their seats and do a self-reflection: thumbs up (I've got it), thumbs sideways (I'm getting it), or thumbs down (I'm having trouble.)

Record of Evidence

Cluster 5:   Successful Learning by All Students

Evidence (cont'd.)

- A two-step word problem will be displayed on the board and read together. Students will discuss how the problem differs from the problems solved during the lesson and possible strategies that could be used to solve it.
- The teacher will explain that in the following lessons they will be working on completing word problems that take multiple steps.

Interpretation

- *The teacher monitors students learning throughout the lesson by asking them to explain their thinking.*

- *The teacher takes into account the students' level of learning, allowing for the use of more concrete strategies for some and more abstract strategies for others, and by honoring all strategies chosen.*

- *The teacher builds into the lesson an opportunity for students to reflect on their own learning and to choose one of two groups for further practice.*

Record of Evidence

Cluster 6:   Professionalism

Guiding Questions

- *To what extent does the teacher engage with the professional community (within the school and beyond) and demonstrate a commitment to ongoing professional learning?*

- *Does the teacher collaborate productively with colleagues and contribute to the life of the school?*

- *Does the teacher engage in professional learning and take a leadership role in the school to promote the welfare of students?*

Evidence

No evidence of Cluster 6 is present in this Instructional Set.

**Looking at Teaching Through
the Lens of the FFT Clusters**

A Study Guide for
Teacher
Learning Communities

Teacher: Nasser
Subject: Social Science
Grade: 9
Topic: Enlightenment/
Text Dependent Questions

Welcome to the Study Guide for the Nasser Social Science Instructional Set, a collection of artifacts and videos for an instructional lesson. This Study Guide provides information and instructions on how to examine teaching and learning through the lens of the Framework for Teaching (FFT) Clusters. In order to complete the steps in this Guide, you will need access to the teacher's planning documents, the lesson video, and the teacher commentary video (http://www.danielsongroup.org/study-guides/). Steps 1–5 of this Study Guide focus on examining the Instructional Set and can be done by an individual. Step 6 is a group activity and focuses on sharing results of the analysis and applications of learning.

Step 1 - Lesson Overview

Read the background information of the lesson provided below.

This text-based lesson continues a unit of study on the Enlightenment. Two sources of written text are being used for this lesson. Source 1 is Immanuel Kant's "What is Enlightenment?" (1784) and Source 2 is Jean Jacques Rousseau's "Emile" (1762). These documents are provided. The teacher supports her rationale for choosing these resources, citing qualitative and quantitative information for each of the two sources. Students read, annotated, analyzed, and discussed three different sources prior to this lesson. Two were nonfiction primary source texts from the Enlightenment. The third source was a video presentation that followed the development of the American education system. Students used these three sources to create challenging text-dependent questions, and then evaluated their complexity. Students were to come to class with their annotated texts and be prepared to respond to classmates' text-dependent questions.

The content objective for this lesson is for students to learn how the Enlightenment can be considered a revolution of thought. The skill objective is for students to be able to effectively provide text-dependent responses to peer-written text-dependent questions. Students are assigned the concept of "Revolution," to which they must connect their responses. They must develop the idea of "Revolution" in relation to the Age of Enlightenment using appropriate selected evidence. Students will work in different settings (pairs, groups, and whole-class) to analyze the authors' claims, purposes, tone, voice, and audiences of the texts. Overall, the students are to draw inferences and conclusions on the relationship between "Revolution" and the Age of Enlightenment, based solely on the texts provided.

Step 2 - Preparation and Questions

- *Read the teacher's lesson plan and jot down things you expect to see and what you want to look for in the video of the lesson.*

- *Write down any questions or comments you have about the lesson plan.*

Step 3 – Viewing the Classroom Video

- *View the complete video, noting those things you expected to see based on the lesson plan. Also note what was missing based on your expectations from the lesson plan. Jot down significant behaviors by the teacher and students pertinent to the FFT Clusters.*

Step 4 – Selected Highlights of the Lesson Video

Read the highlights of the lesson provided below. Note those matching your highlights of the lesson. For each set of statements, determine the FFT Cluster that is best related to the behaviors presented.

In this lesson, Ms. Nasser demonstrates the importance of knowing about her students, and uses this knowledge when planning her lesson. For example, she used her knowledge of the reading proficiency level of each student in the class and their benchmark data to determine student groupings. Ms. Nasser assigned homogeneous group settings for this lesson based on benchmark data she had gathered as well as her own personal observations in the classroom.

A. *No disrespectful interactions from student-to-student or between teacher and students are observed. Students talk respectfully to one another in their small groups. "Yea, maybe," "I know you said that already, right." (1:57-2:10): After a partner shares her opinion, her partner says, "Good job." The student responds, "Thank you." (Cluster ____)*

B. *(8:35): The teacher states: "Here is one model question: 'Which vocabulary word from the text best captures the author's claim?' Take a look at the article. Take a moment and identify with your partner your response to this question. Please identify the word and discuss with your partner." The partners discuss with each other as directed by the teacher. (Cluster ____)*

C. *The teacher immediately begins class by connecting today's work with the previous day's lesson. Students are not talking, but are listening to the teacher as she begins the lesson. (00:34 – 2:15) The teacher says: "First reflect with your partner. I would like you to just take two minutes to discuss those two questions with your partner." Students immediately begin discussing with their partners. Teacher: "Take a few more moments." Teacher walks among students, listening to their discussions. When the teacher calls students back together after partner discussion, they immediately come back to attention. (Cluster ___)*

D. *Students have iPads at their desks when observation begins. Each pair of students has access to at least one iPad. Students are allowed to use their cell phones if they do not have an iPad. Students know the procedure for logging onto their Google accounts. Minimal time is lost while students are logging into their iPads. (Cluster ___)*

E. *The teacher displays the model question on the Smart-Board, has students look at their articles, and then discuss their response with their partners. She has them identify one word to describe their response to the question. She then calls students back to whole-class discussion. She has them share some of their words. Student: "Immaturity." Teacher: "What is the author's claim?" Teacher: "Obstacles, overcoming immaturity. What words did we decide upon?" Student: "Immaturity." Teacher: "Why?" All students participate. (Cluster ___)*

F. *(31:00 – 33:11) The teacher reads the work of three students at the rear of the room to engage students in a discussion and to push their thinking. She then asks questions of these three students about their work. Teacher: "What part of your response do you think connects back to the idea of revolution and change?" Student answers. Teacher: "Excellent, so your idea of revolution is shown by this move to individualization." Student answers. Teacher: "Great! What kind of revolution do you think is associated with enlightenment?" Student answers. Teacher: "What does idealistic mean? Student answers. Teacher: "Umm, okay, so it is a revolution of intellect?"*

Student answers. Teacher: "So it is not something you can see happen?" Student answers. Teacher: "Intellectual, nice, excellent, perfect. You can continue on to category...." (Cluster ___)

G. *Teacher: "Yesterday in class you wrote text-dependent questions, and last night I went through and some of them were really well done and I wish I had written them myself. Some were not as text-dependent; we will be looking at examples today." The teacher does not provide specific feedback explaining why she thought some of their text-dependent questions were good and why some were not as text-dependent. (Cluster ___)*

H. *The teacher circulates during the partner activities to listen to students' discussions as they craft text-dependent responses to peer-generated questions. She monitors and informally assesses student comprehension and engagement. As partners complete their first task, the teacher reads responses from their iPads, asking questions. She sometimes responds to students' answers by providing specific feedback for improvement; other times she provides responses such as "Very good, I like the way you brought metacognition into that;" "good, good;" "fix that second sentence," etc. (Cluster ___)*

Step 5 – Viewing the Teacher Commentary

Watch the video of the teacher's commentary about the lesson and jot down any questions or comments you have about the commentary. Read the highlights below and identify the related FFT Cluster.

A. Ms. Nasser describes what students have been studying prior to this lesson. She explains her process for selecting the texts and the Common Core State Standards (CCSS) goals, based on benchmark data and student observation. Ms. Nasser shares that she had done a Lexile score on the texts to determine how challenging they would be in comparison to the reading levels of the students. She compared this data with the benchmark data from district assessments. Ms. Nasser's planning is clearly purposeful and deliberate. (Cluster ___)

B. Ms. Nasser notes that the students in her class had all enrolled in the World History III honors level class, and share a common interest in history. She explains that even though the students have this shared interest in history, they do not have the same skill level in reading, writing, speaking, and listening. She uses the students' benchmark data to inform her student grouping decisions. Ms. Nasser states that student engagement is her focal point. She uses the Gradual Release Model to show students her thinking and to promote student understanding. She explains her goal is for the students to be challenged, to struggle during the lesson, to be engaged working through that struggle, and to not give up. (Cluster ___)

Step 6 – Questions, Applications, and Discussion

The purpose of this step is to prompt your analysis and reflection of the Instructional Set and to have you think about applications to your own practice.

1. **Teaching and Learning Related to the FFT Clusters**

The purpose of the activity is to increase your understanding of the relationship between the highlights of the Instructional Set and the FFT Clusters. Your identification of an FFT Cluster for each of the highlights is compared to the Cluster identified by the master coders. The Answer Key is located at the end of the activities. You have options on how to complete the comparison. Determine what might work best for your group's learning. Options include, but are not limited to the following.

- Look at the first set of highlights. Take a poll of what each group member identified as the related FFT Cluster. If all members said the same FFT Cluster, have one or two members say why. Compare the group's response to the answer sheet. Repeat for the remainder of the highlights.

OR

- Have each member take one or two highlights. State the correct answer for each one, and a reason why the highlight demonstrates that FFT Cluster. The member will facilitate a discussion if others had different responses, with the goal of having all understand the justification of the correct answer.

OR

- Have members check their own responses to all the highlights. If there are any incorrect answers, then the member selects one highlight and leads a discussion with the group to learn why others think the highlight matches the correct FFT Cluster.

OR

- Determine your own process to check and discuss the match between highlights and the FFT Clusters.

2. Analysis and Reflection of the Instructional Set

The purpose of this activity is for you to analyze and reflect on what you saw and heard in the artifacts and videos, to share your analysis with your peers, and to discuss some of the questions or comments you noted. Review the notes, comments, and questions you recorded when you examined the Instructional Set.

- Identify a key teaching and learning attribute demonstrated in the Instructional Set that was effective and state why you think it worked well.

- Identify a different attribute and provide ideas about how it could be enhanced or improved.

- Share your statements with your group and have your peers react to and build upon your analysis and ideas.

Sample statements:

I noticed the teacher cognitively engaged the majority of the students throughout the lesson. However, the male student in a gray-hooded shirt paired with the female student in a navy blue dress appeared to be off task during the partner activity. He was yawning, fiddling with his hair, and allowing his partner do most of the work. When the teacher was checking their partner work, the conversation was between his female partner and the teacher. This made me want to know more about this student and why he was not actively participating in the activity with his partner. I wondered why the teacher did not engage him in the conversation when checking their partner work. I was curious about how his behavior during this lesson compared with his typical behavior. When I have a student not participating in partner work, I use proximity and ask questions of the student to reengage him/her. If my attempts do not work, I check with others that work or have worked with the student, to see if they have noticed the same behavior and seek their advice. I also check with the student's parents for their insight if the student continues to not participate.

Additional ideas for statements:

- Degree to which students take pride in their work and demonstrate a commitment to mastering challenging content

- Extent to which the instructional strategies used by the teacher are appropriate for the discipline

- Extent to which students monitor their own learning and provide feedback to others

- Extent to which the teacher provides wait time following questions, allowing students time to think and to construct an answer

3. **Notice, Learn, and Apply**

The purpose of this activity is for you to reflect on what you learned from your analysis of the Instructional Set and to determine how you will apply it to your teaching.

- Complete the statements:
  "I noticed _____."
  (Insert one thing you noticed about the teacher or students.)

  "And I learned _____."
  (State what you learned related to what you noticed.)

  "I will apply what I learned by _____."
  (Provide example of how you will use what you learned in your own context.)

- Share your statements with your group. Have others react and add how they might apply what you noticed to their own teaching context.

Sample statement:

- I noticed that when the teacher was checking the work of this particular set of partners, she did not direct any of her questions or comments to the male in the gray-hooded sweatshirt.

- I learned it is important when monitoring student groups to acknowledge and include all group members in the conversation.

- I will apply what I learned by being cognizant of my interactions with individuals in a student group, and will strive to direct questions and comments to all partners in a group.

Study Guide for Teachers Answer Key

Highlights from the Lesson Video (Step 4)

A. No disrespectful interactions from student-to-student or between teacher and students are observed. Students talk respectfully to one another in their small groups. "Yea, maybe," "I know you said that already, right." (1:57-2:10): After a partner shares her opinion, her partner says, "Good job." The student responds, "Thank you." (Cluster 2 Safe, Respectful, Supportive, and Challenging Learning Environment)

B. (8:35): The teacher states: "Here is one model question: 'Which vocabulary word from the text best captures the author's claim?' Take a look at the article. Take a moment and identify with your partner your response to this question. Please identify the word and discuss with your partner." The partners discuss with each other as directed by the teacher. (Cluster 2 Safe, Respectful, Supportive, and Challenging Learning Environment)

C. The teacher immediately begins class by connecting today's work with the previous day's lesson. Students are not talking, but are listening to the teacher as she begins the lesson. (00:34 – 2:15): The teacher says: "First reflect with your partner. I would like you to just take two minutes to discuss those two questions with your partner." Students immediately begin discussing with their partners. Teacher: "Take a few more moments." Teacher walks among students, listening to their discussions. When the teacher calls students back together after partner discussion, they immediately come back to attention. (Cluster 3 Classroom Management)

D. Students have iPads at their desks when observation begins. Each pair of students has access to at least one iPad. Students are allowed to use their cell phones if they do not have an iPad. Students know the procedure for logging onto their Google accounts. Minimal time is lost while students are logging into their iPads. (Cluster 3 Classroom Management)

E. The teacher displays the model question on the SmartBoard, has students look at their articles, and then discuss their response with their partners. She has them identify one word to describe their response to the question. She then calls students back to whole-class discussion. She has them share some of their words. Student: "Immaturity." Teacher: "What is the author's claim?" Teacher: "Obstacles, overcoming immaturity. What words did we decide upon?" Student: "Immaturity." Teacher: "Why?" All students participate. (Cluster 4 Student Intellectual Engagement)

F. (31:00 – 33:11): The teacher reads the work of three students at the rear of the room to engage students in a discussion and to push their thinking. She then asks questions of these three students about their work. Teacher: "What part of your response do you think connects back to the idea of revolution and change?" Student answers. Teacher: "Excellent, so your idea of revolution is shown by this move to individualization." Student answers. Teacher: "Great! What kind of revolution do you think is associated with enlightenment?" Student answers. Teacher: "What does idealistic

Study Guide for Teachers Answer Key

Highlights from the Lesson Video (Step 4—cont'd.)

mean? Student answers. Teacher: "Umm, okay, so it is a revolution of intellect?" Student answers. Teacher: "So it is not something you can see happen?" Student answers. Teacher: "Intellectual, nice, excellent, perfect. You can continue on to category...." (Cluster 4 Student Intellectual Engagement)

G. Teacher: "Yesterday in class you wrote text-dependent questions, and last night I went through and some of them were really well done and I wish I had written them myself. Some were not as text-dependent; we will be looking at examples today." The teacher does not provide specific feedback explaining why she thought some of their text-dependent questions were good and why some were not as text-dependent. (Cluster 5 Successful Learning by All Students)

H. The teacher circulates during the partner activities to listen to students' discussions as they craft text-dependent responses to peer-generated questions. She monitors and informally assesses student comprehension and engagement. As partners complete their first task, the teacher reads responses from their iPads, asking questions. She sometimes responds to students' answers by providing specific feedback for improvement; other times she provides responses such as "Very good, I like the way you brought metacognition into that;" "good, good;" "fix that second sentence," etc. (Cluster 5 Successful Learning by All Students)

Study Guide for Teachers Answer Key

Highlights from the Teacher Commentary (Step 5)

A. Ms. Nasser describes what students have been studying prior to this lesson. She explains her process for selecting the texts and the Common Core State Standards (CCSS) goals, based on benchmark data and student observation. Ms. Nasser shares that she had done a Lexile score on the texts to determine how challenging they would be in comparison to the reading levels of the students. She compared this data with the benchmark data from district assessments. Ms. Nasser's planning is clearly purposeful and deliberate. (Cluster 1 Clarity of Instructional Purpose and Accuracy of Content)

B. Ms. Nasser notes that the students in her class had all enrolled in the World History III honors level class, and share a common interest in history. She explains that even though the students have this shared interest in history, they do not have the same skill level in reading, writing, speaking, and listening. She uses the students' benchmark data to inform her student grouping decisions. Ms. Nasser states that student engagement is her focal point. She uses the Gradual Release Model to show students her thinking and to promote student understanding. She explains her goal is for the students to be challenged, to struggle during the lesson, to be engaged working through that struggle, and to not give up. (Cluster 5 Successful Learning by All Students)

**Looking at Teaching Through
the Lens of the FFT Clusters**

A Study Guide for
Instructional Coach
Learning Communities

Teacher: Nasser
Subject: Social Science
Grade: 9
Topic: Enlightenment/
Text Dependent Questions

Welcome to the Study Guide for the Nasser Social Science Instructional Set, a collection of artifacts and videos for an instructional lesson. This Study Guide provides information and instructions on how to examine teaching and learning through the lens of the Framework for Teaching (FFT) Clusters. In order to complete the steps in this Guide, you will need access to the teacher's planning documents, the lesson video, and the teacher commentary video (http://www.danielsongroup.org/study-guides/). Steps 1–5 of this Study Guide focus on examining the Instructional Set and can be done by an individual. Step 6 is a group activity and focuses on sharing results of the analysis and applications of learning.

Step 1 - Lesson Overview

Read the background information of the lesson provided below.

This text-based lesson continues a unit of study on the Enlightenment. Two sources of written text are being used for this lesson. Source 1 is Immanuel Kant's "What is Enlightenment?" (1784) and Source 2 is Jean Jacques Rousseau's "Emile" (1762). These documents are provided. The teacher supports her rationale for choosing these resources, citing qualitative and quantitative information for each of the two sources. Students read, annotated, analyzed, and discussed three different sources prior to this lesson. Two were nonfiction primary source texts from the Enlightenment. The third source was a video presentation that followed the development of the American education system. Students used these three sources to create challenging text-dependent questions, and then evaluated their complexity. Students were to come to class with their annotated texts and be prepared to respond to classmates' text-dependent questions.

The content objective for this lesson is for students to learn how the Enlightenment can be considered a revolution of thought. The skill objective is for students to be able to effectively provide text-dependent responses to peer-written text-dependent questions. Students are assigned the concept of "Revolution," to which they must connect their responses. They must develop the idea of "Revolution" in relation to the Age of Enlightenment using appropriate selected evidence. Students will work in different settings (pairs, groups, and whole-class) to analyze the authors' claims, purposes, tone, voice, and audiences of the texts. Overall, the students are to draw inferences and conclusions on the relationship between "Revolution" and the Age of Enlightenment, based solely on the texts provided.

Step 2 - Preparation and Questions

- *Read the teacher's lesson plan and jot down things you expect to see and what you want to look for in the video of the lesson.*

- *Write down any questions or comments you have about the lesson plan.*

Step 3 – Viewing the Classroom Video

- *View the complete video, noting those things you expected to see based on the lesson plan. Also note what was missing based on your expectations from the lesson plan. Jot down significant behaviors by the teacher and students pertinent to the FFT Clusters.*

Step 4 – Selected Highlights of the Lesson Video

Read the highlights of the lesson provided below. Note those matching your highlights of the lesson. For each set of statements, determine the FFT Cluster that is best related to the behaviors presented.

In this lesson, Ms. Nasser demonstrates the importance of knowing about her students, and uses this knowledge when planning her lesson. For example, she used her knowledge of the reading proficiency level of each student in the class and their benchmark data to determine student groupings. Ms. Nasser assigned homogeneous group settings for this lesson based on benchmark data she had gathered as well as her own personal observations in the classroom.

A. *No disrespectful interactions from student-to-student or between teacher and students are observed. Students talk respectfully to one another in their small groups. "Yea, maybe," "I know you said that already, right." (1:57-2:10): After a partner shares her opinion, her partner says, "Good job." The student responds, "Thank you." (Cluster ____)*

B. *(8:35): The teacher states: "Here is one model question: 'Which vocabulary word from the text best captures the author's claim?' Take a look at the article. Take a moment and identify with your partner your response to this question. Please identify the word and discuss with your partner." The partners discuss with each other as directed by the teacher. (Cluster ____)*

C. *The teacher immediately begins class by connecting to-day's work with the previous day's lesson. Students are not talking, but are listening to the teacher as she begins the lesson. (00:34 – 2:15) The teacher says: "First reflect with your partner. I would like you to just take two minutes to discuss those two questions with your partner." Students immediately begin discussing with their partners. Teacher: "Take a few more moments." Teacher walks among students, listening to their discussions. When the teacher calls students back together after partner discussion, they immediately come back to attention. (Cluster ____)*

D. *Students have iPads at their desks when observation begins. Each pair of students has access to at least one iPad. Students are allowed to use their cell phones if they do not have an iPad. Students know the procedure for logging onto their Google accounts. Minimal time is lost while students are logging into their iPads. (Cluster ____)*

E. *The teacher displays the model question on the Smart-Board, has students look at their articles, and then discuss their response with their partners. She has them identify one word to describe their response to the question. She then calls students back to whole-class discussion. She has them share some of their words. Student: "Immaturity." Teacher: "What is the author's claim?" Teacher: "Obstacles, overcoming immaturity. What words did we decide upon?" Student: "Immaturity." Teacher: "Why?" All students participate. (Cluster ____)*

F. *(31:00 – 33:11) The teacher reads the work of three students at the rear of the room to engage students in a discussion and to push their thinking. She then asks questions of these three students about their work. Teacher: "What part of your response do you think connects back to the idea of revolution and change?" Student answers. Teacher: "Excellent, so your idea of revolution is shown by this move to individualization." Student answers. Teacher: "Great! What kind of revolution do you think is associated with enlightenment?" Student answers. Teacher: "What does idealistic mean? Student answers. Teacher: "Umm, okay, so it is a revolution of intellect?"*

Student answers. Teacher: "So it is not something you can see happen?" Student answers. Teacher: "Intellectual, nice, excellent, perfect. You can continue on to category...." (Cluster ____)

G. *Teacher: "Yesterday in class you wrote text-dependent questions, and last night I went through and some of them were really well done and I wish I had written them myself. Some were not as text-dependent; we will be looking at examples today." The teacher does not provide specific feedback explaining why she thought some of their text-dependent questions were good and why some were not as text-dependent. (Cluster ____)*

H. *The teacher circulates during the partner activities to listen to students' discussions as they craft text-dependent responses to peer-generated questions. She monitors and informally assesses student comprehension and engagement. As partners complete their first task, the teacher reads responses from their iPads, asking questions. She sometimes responds to students' answers by providing specific feedback for improvement; other times she provides responses such as "Very good, I like the way you brought metacognition into that;" "good, good;" "fix that second sentence," etc. (Cluster ____)*

Step 5 – Viewing the Teacher Commentary

Watch the video of the teacher's commentary about the lesson and jot down any questions or comments you have about the commentary. Read the highlights below and identify the related FFT Cluster.

A. Ms. Nasser describes what students have been studying prior to this lesson. She explains her process for selecting the texts and the Common Core State Standards (CCSS) goals, based on benchmark data and student observation. Ms. Nasser shares that she had done a Lexile score on the texts to determine how challenging they would be in comparison to the reading levels of the students. She compared this data with the benchmark data from district assessments. Ms. Nasser's planning is clearly purposeful and deliberate. (Cluster ___)

B. Ms. Nasser notes that the students in her class had all enrolled in the World History III honors level class, and share a common interest in history. She explains that even though the students have this shared interest in history, they do not have the same skill level in reading, writing, speaking, and listening. She uses the students' benchmark data to inform her student grouping decisions. Ms. Nasser states that student engagement is her focal point. She uses the Gradual Release Model to show students her thinking and to promote student understanding. She explains her goal is for the students to be challenged, to struggle during the lesson, to be engaged working through that struggle, and to not give up. (Cluster ___)

6

Step 6 – Questions, Applications, and Discussion

The purpose of this step is to prompt your analysis and reflection of the Instructional Set and to have you think about applications to your own practice.

1. Teaching and Learning Related to the FFT Clusters

The purpose of the activity is to increase your understanding of the relationship between the highlights of the Instructional Set and the FFT Clusters. Your identification of an FFT Cluster for each of the highlights is compared to the Cluster identified by the master coders. The Answer Key is located at the end of the activities. You have options on how to complete the comparison. Determine what might work best for your group's learning. Options include, but are not limited to the following.

- Look at the first set of highlights. Take a poll of what each group member identified as the related FFT Cluster. If all members said the same FFT Cluster, then have one or two members say why. Compare the group's response to the answer sheet. Repeat for the remainder of the sets of highlights.

OR

- Have each member take one or two sets of highlights and be the discussant for them. The discussant will state the correct answer and state a reason why the statements in the set demonstrate the FFT Cluster. The discussant will facilitate a discussion if members had different responses with the goal of all understanding the justification of the correct answer.

OR

- Have members check their own responses to all the sets of highlights. If there are any incorrect answers, then the member selects one set and leads a discussion with the group to learn why others think the highlights match the correct FFT Cluster.

OR

- Determine your own process to check and discuss the match between highlights and the FFT Clusters.

2. Analysis and Reflection of the Instructional Set

The purpose of this activity is for you to analyze and reflect on what you saw and heard in the artifacts and videos and to discuss some of the questions or comments you noted. One element of a professional conversation is asking questions to ascertain more information about a teacher's thinking and the behaviors of both students and teacher. This activity allows you and your peers to practice preparing such questions. Your peers can comment on whether your questions are appropriate and will obtain useful information without making the featured teacher feel uneasy or criticized.

The second part of this activity focuses on helping teachers move their practice forward. Please note that having you prepare for and model an entire conversation about the lesson with the featured teacher is not the purpose of this activity as written. Your group can modify or replace the activity to meet your group's needs

- Review the notes, comments, and questions you recorded when you examined the Instructional Set. Pretend you have the opportunity to ask the teacher some questions to get additional information about the strategies used or decisions made for this Instructional Set.

- Share with your group just the questions you would use with the teacher to elicit additional information. Have your peers comment about your questions and add other questions they had about the same event.

- Share with others in your group what you would do to prompt the teacher's thinking and actions to enhance his/her practice. Take turns sharing and discussing the prompts.

Sample A, Part I:

You monitored students' learning by asking open-ended questions during both the whole group discussion and the partner activity. You walked around the classroom to each set of partners, read their group work on their iPads, and asked questions to solicit their understanding of their work. Two samples of feedback you gave to students included:

1. "One thing you need to add in to that is the concept of revolution or change. So you can either add as an extra ending, or as an opening, or an analysis statement."

2. "For the most part, your questions did not use background knowledge; there were a few that may have asked opinions that would have required oral background knowledge."

In these two examples of feedback, it appears you are doing all of the work and learning. What might be some changes you could possibly make to your feedback to cause the students to have to suggest ways to improve their work? For example, when you provide feedback such as "excellent, perfect, and well-done," you might try, "Can you tell me why I might consider that statement excellent?" to get the students to think and take action?

Sample A, Part II:

Ms. Nasser, you noted in your lesson plans your intention to differentiate instruction for individuals or groups of students in the class, based on their benchmark assessment scores and your general observations, by scaffolding the analyses of the texts for students needing more supports. You placed students in mixed-ability pairs for crafting text-dependent responses. You selected the pairs by reviewing individual student strengths, and then pairing those who were strong in the skills needed for this activity with those students who might need further development. In reflecting on this lesson, what are some of your thoughts about the success of this differentiation for individuals or groups? What changes might you consider for future partner work?

Sample B, Part I:

Ms. Nasser, during closing, you instructed the students to take out a piece of lined paper and said, "You have spent a lot of time looking at what enlightenment means. Respond to this one question: 'What kind of revolution was the Enlightenment?' " After you repeated the question, the students began to write. You also told them to just write their opinion, because they did not have time to use text-dependent evidence to answer the question. The bell rang as they were completing their opinions on the lined paper. For those students who may not have finished, what were the options they had for completing the task? In reflecting on your lesson outline, what might be some things you would consider changing to allow students more time to complete the summative assessment?

Sample B, Part II:

What areas of success or weakness did you notice about their opinions, based on the responses of the class as a whole? What examples of successful opinions come to mind that informed your conclusion? What might be some plans or ideas you have in mind next to promote the understanding of this lesson for those partners who may have not been as successful as others?

3. **Notice, Learn, and Apply**

The purpose of this activity is for you to reflect on what you learned from your analysis of the Instructional Set and to determine how you will apply it to your teaching.

- Complete the statements:
  "I noticed _____."
  (Insert one thing you noticed about the teacher or students.)

  "And I learned _____."
  (State what you learned related to what you noticed.)

  "I will apply what I learned by _____."
  (Provide example of how you will use what you learned in your own context.)

- Share your statements with your group. Have others react and add how they might apply what you noticed to their own coaching context.

Sample statements:

- I noticed the teacher had the students individually give their opinion to one strategic question: "What kind of revolution was the Enlightenment?"

- I learned that choosing a strategic question is a quick and effective way to check the understanding of individual students.

- I will apply what I learned by sharing this strategy with other teachers that I'm coaching, especially when their lesson involves a lot of partner work.

Study Guide for Instructional Coaches Answer Key
Highlights from the Lesson Video (Step 4)

A. No disrespectful interactions from student-to-student or between teacher and students are observed. Students talk respectfully to one another in their small groups. "Yea, maybe," "I know you said that already, right." (1:57-2:10): After a partner shares her opinion, her partner says, "Good job." The student responds, "Thank you." (Cluster 2 Safe, Respectful, Supportive, and Challenging Learning Environment)

B. (8:35): The teacher states: "Here is one model question: 'Which vocabulary word from the text best captures the author's claim?' Take a look at the article. Take a moment and identify with your partner your response to this question. Please identify the word and discuss with your partner." The partners discuss with each other as directed by the teacher. (Cluster 2 Safe, Respectful, Supportive, and Challenging Learning Environment)

C. The teacher immediately begins class by connecting today's work with the previous day's lesson. Students are not talking, but are listening to the teacher as she begins the lesson. (00:34 – 2:15): The teacher says: "First reflect with your partner. I would like you to just take two minutes to discuss those two questions with your partner." Students immediately begin discussing with their partners. Teacher: "Take a few more moments." Teacher walks among students, listening to their discussions. When the teacher calls students back together after partner discussion, they immediately come back to attention. (Cluster 3 Classroom Management)

D. Students have iPads at their desks when observation begins. Each pair of students has access to at least one iPad. Students are allowed to use their cell phones if they do not have an iPad. Students know the procedure for logging onto their Google accounts. Minimal time is lost while students are logging into their iPads. (Cluster 3 Classroom Management)

E. The teacher displays the model question on the SmartBoard, has students look at their articles, and then discuss their response with their partners. She has them identify one word to describe their response to the question. She then calls students back to whole-class discussion. She has them share some of their words. Student: "Immaturity." Teacher: "What is the author's claim?" Teacher: "Obstacles, overcoming immaturity. What words did we decide upon?" Student: "Immaturity." Teacher: "Why?" All students participate. (Cluster 4 Student Intellectual Engagement)

F. (31:00 – 33:11): The teacher reads the work of three students at the rear of the room to engage students in a discussion and to push their thinking. She then asks questions of these three students about their work. Teacher: "What part of your response do you think connects back to the idea of revolution and change?" Student answers. Teacher: "Excellent, so your idea of revolution is shown by this move to individualization." Student answers. Teacher: "Great! What kind of revolution do you think is associated with enlightenment?" Student answers. Teacher: "What does idealistic mean? Student answers. Teacher: "Umm, okay, so it is a revolution of intellect?" Student answers. Teacher: "So it is not something you can see happen?" Student answers. Teacher: "Intellectual, nice, excellent, perfect. You can continue on to category...." (Cluster 4 Student Intellectual Engagement)

G. Teacher: "Yesterday in class you wrote text-dependent questions, and last night I went through and some of them were really well done and I wish I had written them myself. Some were not as text-dependent; we will be looking at examples today." The teacher does not provide specific feedback explaining why she thought some of their text-dependent questions were good and why some were not as text-dependent. (Cluster 5 Successful Learning by All Students)

H. The teacher circulates during the partner activities to listen to students' discussions as they craft text-dependent responses to peer-generated questions. She monitors and informally assesses student comprehension and engagement. As partners complete their first task, the teacher reads responses from their iPads, asking questions. She sometimes responds to students' answers by providing specific feedback for improvement; other times she provides responses such as "Very good, I like the way you brought metacognition into that;" "good, good;" "fix that second sentence," etc. (Cluster 5 Successful Learning by All Students)

Study Guide for Instructional Coaches Answer Key
Highlights from the Teacher Commentary (Step 5)

A. Ms. Nasser describes what students have been studying prior to this lesson. She explains her process for selecting the texts and the Common Core State Standards (CCSS) goals, based on benchmark data and student observation. Ms. Nasser shares that she had done a Lexile score on the texts to determine how challenging they would be in comparison to the reading levels of the students. She compared this data with the benchmark data from district assessments. Ms. Nasser's planning is clearly purposeful and deliberate. (Cluster 1 Clarity of Instructional Purpose and Accuracy of Content)

B. Ms. Nasser notes that the students in her class had all enrolled in the World History III honors level class, and share a common interest in history. She explains that even though the students have this shared interest in history, they do not have the same skill level in reading, writing, speaking, and listening. She uses the students' benchmark data to inform her student grouping decisions. Ms. Nasser states that student engagement is her focal point. She uses the Gradual Release Model to show students her thinking and to promote student understanding. She explains her goal is for the students to be challenged, to struggle during the lesson, to be engaged working through that struggle, and to not give up. (Cluster 5 Successful Learning by All Students)

Record of Evidence

This Record of Evidence (ROE) contains key evidence aligned to the FFT Clusters. Interpretive statements about the evidence are also provided. The ROE was created by two master coders who recorded evidence and interpretation statements independently, reviewed each others' work, and arrived at a final composite version based on their professional conversations. This version was reviewed by a leader of the master coders. The ROE is included in this Study Guide so users can see what master coders identified as key evidence, and their interpretation of that evidence through the lens of the FFT Clusters. It is provided as an example of one type of analysis of an Instructional Set. The ROEs were created for professional development rather than evaluative purposes. Users are cautioned about using them for teacher evaluation.

Rubric:	Generic
Grade:	9
Subject:	Social Science
Topic:	Enlightenment/Text Dependent Questions
Teacher description:	Female, caucasian, experience unknown
Class description:	21 students. Quote from #6 on the Interview Protocol for a Pre-Observation (Planning) Conference document: "The students in this Honors World History course are motivated individuals with a shared interest. Yet, although they are advanced in comparison to some of their peers in grade 9, they all still have very different strengths and weaknesses. There are a few students needing accommodations, such as extended time and further scaffolding on assignments. In designing this lesson and the days leading up to this point, there were a few contributing factors to my decisions in group and pair assignments and the learning activities. In addition to my own observations and assessments, I reviewed the district data of benchmark assessments over the past year to gain a better understanding of my students' abilities. I learned that, in regards to the skills embedded within reading and writing, the students ranged widely. Also, a sampling of the students in this Honors level class qualifies for the free/reduced lunch program, indicative of the socioeconomic gap within the room.

Record of Evidence

Artifacts:
- Interview Protocol for a Pre-observation (Planning Conference)
- Helmsley Lesson on Enlightenment Checklist
- Text- Dependent Question Stems
- Three samples of students' work
- Student handouts: Crafting-Text-Dependent Questions, Checklist for Evaluating Question Quality, and Source #1 and Source #2 – The Enlightenment

Length of video: 40:12

Cluster 1:   Clarity of Instructional Purpose and Accuracy of Content

Guiding Questions

- *To what extent does the teacher demonstrate depth of important content knowledge and conduct the class with a clear and ambitious purpose, reflective of the standards for the discipline and appropriate to the students' levels of knowledge and skill?*

- *To what degree are the elements of a lesson (the sequence of topics, instructional strategies, and materials and resources) well designed and executed, and aligned with the purpose of the lesson?*

- *To what extent are they designed to engage students in high-level learning in the discipline?*

Record of Evidence

Cluster 1: Clarity of Instructional Purpose and Accuracy of Content

Evidence

Instructional Plan
- Explanation of how the lesson will address one CCSS ELA-Literacy/World History standard and two CCSS ELA standards.
- Information prior to today's lesson and what students will do next after this lesson: "peer-evaluate the text-dependent responses using the criteria rehearsed in class."
- Two lesson objectives:
  1. *Content Objective*: Students will learn how the Enlightenment can be considered a revolution of thought.
  2. *Skill Objective*: Students will learn to effectively provide text-dependent responses to peer-written text-dependent questions.
- Materials and instructional resources:
  1. (Written text) Immanuel Kant's "What is Enlightenment?"
  2. (Written text) Jean Jacques Rousseau's "Emile"
- The teacher provides her rationale for choosing these resources, citing qualitative and quantitative information for each source.
- How the learning fits into the following is critical to understanding the next unit on the French Revolution:
  - the sequence of learning
  - the curriculum for the school's mission
  - the 9th grade social studies curriculum
- A structure is included for how students will be engaged in the lesson: Preparation, Initiation, Lesson Development, and Closure.
- Description of the students in this class, including those with special needs.
- The teacher gives explanation of how she grouped the students for this lesson and how she will differentiate for the students based on that grouping. The teacher indicates where she thinks the students will struggle during the lesson, and this was evident during the video.
- Plans for student assessment: The lesson states that the students will evaluate their own individual progress towards meeting the content and skills objective, however, this is not observed during the video.
- There is a checklist (that has been provided to the students) for evaluating question quality.

Artifacts
- Interview Protocol for a Pre-observation (Planning Conference)
- Helmsley Lesson on Enlightenment Checklist
- Text-Dependent Question Stems
- Three samples of students' work
- Student handouts: Crafting-Text-Dependent Questions, Checklist for Evaluating Question Quality and Source #1 and Source #2—The Enlightenment

Record of Evidence

Cluster 1: Clarity of Instructional Purpose and Accuracy of Content

Evidence (cont'd.)

Teacher Commentary
- The teacher states that student engagement is her focal point. The teacher states, "Engagement is not how fun a lesson is, it's not that the kids are smiling and laughing, it is that the students feel challenged and they want to engage in the lesson. They want to struggle and they are working through it and not giving up; that is engagement."
- She begins by first looking at past texts that were nonfiction and also rich in vocabulary to identify the text(s) that will be most appropriate for the students. She did a Lexile score on the texts to determine how challenging those texts would be in comparison to the reading levels of the students. The teacher also compares this data with the benchmark data from district assessments.
- The teacher notes that the students in her class are enrolled in the honors level World History III class and share a common interest in history. She explains that even though the students have this shared interest in history, they do not have the same skill levels in reading, writing, speaking, and listening. She uses the students' benchmark data to inform her decision when assigning them to different groups.
- The teacher summarizes that she assigned homogeneous groups using both benchmark data and her own personal observations in the classroom.

Video
- The teacher begins the lesson by sharing that yesterday they wrote text-dependent questions, and the previous night she had reviewed them and found that some were well done, but others were not as text-dependent. She states they will be looking at examples today. She has students reflect with their partners on two questions: 1) What challenges did you face in writing text-dependent questions, and 2) What is the value in writing text-dependent questions? After partners discuss for two minutes, the teacher calls on some students to share their challenges and struggles with the class.
- The teacher discusses today's two objectives with the whole class. The objectives are written on the board. She tells the students that today they are going to be responding to some of the text-dependent questions. She explains to students that she has identified two from each of the sources they had written that she thought were excellent, and she is sharing these with two other students within the classroom. She explains today they will not be seeing or answering their own questions. Today they will be answering someone else's questions from class.
- The teacher has students log in to Google Docs. Teacher reviews elements of a text-dependent response using a text-dependent question example on the Smart-Board. The teacher models a response. Students share qualities of a strong text-dependent response.

Record of Evidence

Cluster 1:   Clarity of Instructional Purpose and Accuracy of Content

Evidence (cont'd.)

- The teacher gives instructions for pair work. As the students work with their partners, the teacher walks among the desks, reading their work, asking questions, and making suggestions for improvement.
- The teacher has students get out a piece of lined paper and answer the following question as a closing activity: "What kind of revolution was the Enlightenment?" Students spend the remainder of class time writing their answers. She tells them she wants them to write down their opinions and not to use text-dependent responses.

Interpretation

- The lesson objectives, materials, sequence, etc. are important for World History.

- Appropriate and detailed activities are scaffolded and support the achievement of the objectives.

- The teacher's instructional plan is thorough and indicates she is clear about what students are going to do to meet the learning goals in this lesson.

- The teacher's explanation about how text fits in the sequence of learning for this class, and the questions she plans to use, demonstrate her knowledge of the text and her use of text to support students' learning.

- The teacher's planning appears to be thorough and sequential based on:
  - her explanation of what students have been studying
  - her process for selecting the CCSS goals and texts based on benchmark data and student observations
  - her process for assigning student groupings
  - her use of the Gradual Release Model to show students her thinking.

- The teacher's reflection indicates that she is very detailed in her organizational planning for this lesson.

- No content errors are noted in the planing or delivery of instruction.

- It is not certain if the students understand what they will be learning during this lesson, as the teacher merely has a student read the outcome and then says "very good."

Record of Evidence

Cluster 2: Safe, Respectful, Supportive, and Challenging Learning Environment

Guiding Questions

- *To what extent do the interactions between teacher and students, and among students, demonstrate genuine caring and a safe, respectful, supportive, and also challenging learning environment?*

- *Do teachers convey high expectations for student learning and encourage hard work and perseverance? Is the environment safe for risk taking?*

- *Do students take pride in their work and demonstrate a commitment to mastering challenging content?*

Evidence

- Ms. Nasser calls the students by name, and students are willing to respond when called upon.

- No disrespectful talk or interactions are observed between teacher and students nor among the students. Students talk respectfully to one another in their small groups. "Yea, maybe," "I know you said that already, right."

- (1:57-2:10) After a student states her opinion, her partner says, "Good job." The student responds, "Thank you."

- The teacher responds to students' explanations using words such as "nice, excellent, perfect, well-done, very specific, very detailed" during the partner activity.

- The teacher conveys high expectations for student learning from the very beginning to the end of the lesson. She begins the lesson by connecting homework and text-related work from the previous day to explain her expectations for today's lesson. She ensures students understanding of her expectations by telling them what they are going to do, relating it to previous or current learning, asking questions, and then using students' answers to both monitor for student understanding and to clarify and explain activities. She repeats this process when sharing expectations for all activities during the lesson.

- (6:00) T: Today we are going to be responding to some of the text-dependent questions. I went through and a lot of yours were really awesome questions. I identified two from each of the sources that you wrote that I thought were excellent and then I shared with two other people within the classroom, so you will not be seeing or answering your own questions. Today, you will be answering someone else's questions from class, and you will see whose they are so that you can give props to them for writing these questions.

- T: I'll help you if you have questions.

Record of Evidence

Cluster 2: Safe, Respectful, Supportive, and Challenging Learning Environment

Evidence (cont'd.)

- Teacher circulates during the partner activity, listening to students as they share with each other, asking questions, and providing feedback with suggestions for improving their responses.

- (8:35) T: Here is one model question: "Which vocabulary word from the text best captures the author's claim?" Take a look at the article… Take a moment and identify with your partner your response to this question. Please identify the word and discuss with your partner. The partners discuss with each other as directed by the teacher.

- Most students share their ideas freely during the class discussion.

- Students appear to be at ease in sharing ideas and opinions during the partner activity.

- One pair (two girls) struggles with the correct words but perseveres.

- (34:17) Another pair of girls perseveres through answering one of the questions.

Interpretation

- The only parts difficult to discern are students taking pride in their work and visual confirmation that students are committed to mastering the challenging content.

- Students complete the assignment, but high levels of cognitive energy is difficult to discern.

- There is no indication that minds were being changed or interpretations modified as a result of the discussion, with the exception of the teacher telling one group who asked about context that Langston Hughes was black.

Record of Evidence

Cluster 3:   Classroom Management

Guiding Questions

- *Is the classroom well run and organized?*

- *Are classroom routines and procedures clear and carried out efficiently by both teacher and students with little loss of instructional time?*

- *To what extent do students themselves take an active role in their smooth operation?*

- *Are directions for activities clearly explained so that there is no confusion?*

- *Do students not only understand and comply with standards of conduct, but also play an active part in setting the tone for maintaining those standards?*

- *How does the physical environment support the learning activities?*

Evidence
- Teacher immediately begins class by connecting today's work with the previous day's lesson. Students are not talking, and listen to the teacher as she begins the lesson.
- (00:34 – 2:15) T: First reflect with your partner…. I would like you to just take two minutes to discuss those two questions with your partner. Students immediately begin discussing with their partners.
- T: Take a few more moments. Teacher walks among students, listening to their discussions.
- When teacher calls students back together after partner discussion, students immediately come back to attention.
- Students are sitting with assigned partners in desks arranged in sets of two and one set of three when the observation begins. The seating arrangement provides visibility to teacher and each other, as well as the SmartBoard and the board. The desks are arranged for students to be able to talk with their partners.
- The two objectives and "Do Now" questions are written on the board when the observation begins.
- Students have iPads at their desks. Each pair of students has access to at least one iPad. Students are allowed to use their cell phones if they do not have an iPad. Students know the procedure for logging in to their Google accounts. Minimal time is lost while students are logging in to their iPads.
- Students immediately become silent when teacher calls them to attention to talk about transitioning. Transitions, from whole group discussion to partner activity and from partner activity to whole group discussion, take less than a minute.
- The behavior of the students is appropriate. The teacher does not have to re-direct any student.

Record of Evidence

Cluster 3:   Classroom Management

Evidence (cont'd.)

- As students are logging in, the teacher turns on the SmartBoard to display the model question and responses. The model question and responses are already on the SmartBoard when it comes on.
- Teacher asks questions, then listens and builds on students' answers when explaining directions for the day's activities.
- Teacher alerts students by indicating how much time they have to complete a task.
- Most students are productive and make good use of time.
- Students raise a hand before speaking throughout the class discussion.
- One girl has trouble logging out of her Google account near the end of the lesson. The teacher also encounters a problem when assisting the girl. Her partner explains to the girl and the teacher how she goes to Google and signs out from there.
- No paraprofessional or volunteer is observed in the classroom.

Interpretation

- This classroom runs smoothly, with little loss of instructional time.

- Materials are already in place when lesson begins (e.g., text on SmartBoard, iPads, lined paper, student handouts).

- The classroom is arranged to support the learning that is done in pairs. The distance between desks allows teacher to move freely among the desks when monitoring.

- The teacher provides directions for each of the activities. Most students appear to understand the directions for the activities. Occasionally the teacher has to explain the directions to some partners.

- Students appear to be well-behaved. Talking stops when the teacher calls them back to whole group. When the teacher tells them to discuss with their partners, they follow her requests.

- The teacher and one partner accept the assistance of the other partner about how to sign out from Google.

Record of Evidence

Cluster 4: Student Intellectual Engagement

Guiding Questions

- *To what extent are students intellectually engaged in a classroom of high intellectual energy?*

- *What is the nature of what students are doing?*

- *Are they being challenged to think and make connections through both the instructional activities and the questions explored?*

- *Do the teacher's explanations of content correctly model academic language and invite intellectual work by students?*

- *Are students asked to explain their thinking, to construct logical arguments citing evidence, and to question the thinking of others?*

- *Are the instructional strategies used by the teacher suitable to the discipline, and to what extent do they promote student agency in the learning of challenging content?*

Evidence

- Teacher begins by connecting previous day's lesson to what they will do today.
- The teacher assigns students a "Do Now" activity. She points to the two questions on the board while explaining the directions for the activity.
- T: Before we get into that, I would like for you to reflect with your partner on these two questions: 1) What challenges did you face in writing text-dependent questions and 2) What is the value in writing text-dependent questions? Discuss these with your partner. The partners discuss the two questions.
- (2:14) T: What challenges did you face in writing text-dependent questions? Some people struggled, so what were those struggles? Kelley?
- S: Making sure your text-dependent questions were really text-dependent and did not use background knowledge.
- (2:30) T: For the most part, your questions did not use background knowledge; there were a few that may have asked opinions that would have required oral background knowledge.
- S: We had to make sure that we weren't repetitive so that we weren't asking the same questions over and over again.
- T: There were six questions you had to write for each source. That is challenging because one main idea, how do you really stand behind that claim?
- S: I found that a lot of my questions were not conceptual and they were a lot of my opinion, rather than trying to analyze what he is actually saying.
- T: How did you fix these questions?
- S: I fixed them by trying to eliminate anything that is not actually in the text.
- (3:45) S: We had to make it sound normal and sophisticated, but at the same time, make sense.
- (4:30) S: You had to make sure it was relative and important to the claim or objective.

Record of Evidence

Cluster 4: Student Intellectual Engagement

Evidence (cont'd.)

- S: The generating question wasn't as hard, but making it back to the content objective and making sure it was relevant to what we were actually learning.
- T: So what is the value? Why ask text-dependent questions?
- S: It opens up new doors for understanding the text if you write down text-dependent questions. It makes you think a little deeper about what you are really trying to get, like the objective or the claim.
- T: What else did you learn?
- S: It helps you become a better writer.
- T: (giving directions for the partner activity): Today we are going to be responding to some of the text-dependent questions. I went through, and a lot of yours were really awesome questions. I identified two from each of the sources that you wrote that I thought were excellent and then I shared with two other people within the classroom, so you will not be seeing or answering your own questions. Today you will be answering someone else's questions from class, and you will see whose they are so that you can give props to them for writing good questions."
- Teacher has students log in to Google on their iPads. While they are logging in, she turns on the SmartBoard and says that she is going to show them a few questions she thought were strong text-dependent questions; they will review what is good about them.
- Before showing the model question on the SmartBoard, the teacher restates the two objectives. She explains to students they are going to learn how enlightenment can be considered a revolution. She says that in the past, she had them streamline their annotations so they aligned with the objective, and check to see if they matched the author's claim. She explains that today they will streamline their responses to match a concept by connecting their responses to the idea of revolution.
- The teacher displays the model question on the SmartBoard, and has the students look at their article and discuss their response with their partners. She asks them to identify one word to describe their response to the question. She then calls students back to a whole class discussion. She has them share some of their words. S: Immaturity. T: What is the author's claim? T: Obstacles, overcoming immaturity. What words did we decide upon? S: Immaturity. T: Why?
- The teacher tells the partners to open the document she has sent them with the text-dependent questions.
- (16:56) Students (trio) are talking about the questions. Two girls in front are not talking to one another. Most students appear to be working on the task without any hesitation.
- The teacher circulates throughout the classroom, observing and listening to the students' conversation. Instead of interrupting students, she listens to their conversation. As students finish their first question, the teacher reads the responses on their iPads, asking questions and providing suggestions for improvement, such as:

Record of Evidence

Cluster 4: Student Intellectual Engagement

Evidence (cont'd.)

- (25:30) T: You might want to fix that. Teacher talks to the female and not to the male partner. T: My only concern is to achieve enlightenment sounds a little bit repetitive. The conversation is between teacher and the female partner. There is no discussion between the male partner and the teacher.
- (27:57) T: One thing you need to add in to that is the concept of revolution or change. So you can either as an extra ending or as an opening or an analysis statement. You can add this as a closing of your sentence or incorporate into an analysis.
- (31:00–33:11) Teacher reads work of three students at rear of room T: What part of your response do you think connects back to the idea of revolution and change? Student answers. T: Excellent, so your idea of revolution is shown by this move to individualization. Student answers. T: Great! What kind of revolution do you think is associated with enlightenment? Student answers. T: What does idealistic mean? Student answers. T: Umm, okay, so it is a revolution of intellect? Student answers. T: So it is not something you can see happen. Student answers. T: Intellectual, nice, excellent, perfect. You can continue on to category...."
- (35:06) T: Ladies and gentlemen, I would like for you to pause what you are doing... and this has been done on Google docs and automatically saves. We will continue to work on this on Monday. You will finish up your questions. I would like you to log out of your Google doc account. Close your questions.
- (37:19) T: I'd like you to respond to this question: "What kind of revolution was the Enlightenment?" I just want your reaction.

Record of Evidence

Cluster 4: Student Intellectual Engagement

Interpretation

- The teacher immediately begins the lesson and commends students for their text-dependent questions by telling them she wishes she had written them herself.

- The students had choice in developing text-dependent questions. As they answer text-dependent questions that are not their own, they have choice as to which quotes will support their claims.

- The teacher consistently asks students to defend their answers and to make connections to the Enlightenment revolution.

- A sampling of students' responses from the "Do Now" activity reflects students' higher-level thinking.

- There is some modeling of the process, but no conversation amongst the students after the teacher has modeled. This led to some confusion on the students' part as to what they were to accomplish.

- The partnering activity appears to present a productive struggle for students. Most of the time, the teacher doesn't give answers, but uses prodding to help students find their own answers.

- Most students appear to be engaged during the partner activity, with the exception of one male student in a gray-hooded shirt who sometimes appear disengaged (paired with the female student in a navy blue dress).

- All of the activities in the lesson require higher-level thinking and are intellectually challenging.

- The teacher promotes student initiative when she tells some students what she likes about the answers they gave while speaking or on their iPads.

- The teacher does not direct her conversation to the male student in the gray-hooded shirt when checking partner work. All of the conversation is between his female partner in the navy blue dress and the teacher.

- Students seem to accept the teacher's suggestions for making improvements to their responses.

- The bell rings as the students are completing their opinions on the lined paper.

Record of Evidence

Cluster 5:   Successful Learning by All Students

Guiding Questions

- *To what extent does the teacher ensure learning by all students?*

- *Does the teacher monitor student understanding through specifically designed questions or instructional techniques?*

- *To what extent do students monitor their own learning and provide respectful feedback to classmates?*

- *Does the teacher make modifications in presentations or learning activities where necessary, taking into account the degree of student learning?*

- *Has the teacher sought out other resources (including parents) to support students' learning?*

- *In reflection, is the teacher aware of the success of the lesson in reaching students?*

Evidence

- Learning outcomes aligned with CCSS are provided in the lesson plan. The teacher plans for all students to participate in the activities. Teacher has heterogeneously paired the students. The lesson plan states she will implement the Gradual Release Method. She monitors throughout the lesson, asking questions and listening to students' responses or reading them on their iPads. All pairs and one trio have access to at least one iPad to use during the lesson.
- T: Yesterday in class you wrote text-dependent questions and last night I went through and some of them were really well done and I wish I had written them myself. Some were not as text-dependent; we will be looking at examples today. The teacher does not provide feedback explaining to students why she thought their text-dependent questions were good.
- The teacher monitors students' understanding during whole group discussions by sharing her thoughts, asking questions, and listening to students' responses. The teacher often provides feedback in the form of probing questions or making suggestions for improvement.
- Students craft text-dependent responses to peer-generated questions during the partner activities. The teacher circulates to monitor and informally assess student comprehension and engagement. As partners complete their first task, Ms. Nasser reads their responses from their iPads, asks questions, and responds to students answers. She sometimes provides specific feedback for improvement, and other times provides responses such as "Very good, I like the way you brought metacognition into that. Good, good. Fix that second sentence."
- Teacher monitors by walking around from 18:45–21:39. The teacher is not seen or heard responding to any group.

Record of Evidence

Cluster 5:   Successful Learning by All Students

Evidence (cont'd.)

- T: Perfect, you have to know what the claim is and then the word and connect these two. Why do you think this is a good text-dependent question?
- S: It makes the reader go back to what the claim is and then connect it with what the author was trying to convey.
- T: How would you answer this question? What do you need to include in your response to make it good response? Think back to an acronym we have practiced.
- (22:57) T: I also saw that you used a synonym for revolution. Do you know what it was? Which is totally fine that you did that. What was it?
- S: Change?
- T: Change, perfect, very good.
- In closing, the teacher instructs students to take out a piece of lined paper. T: You have spent a lot of time looking at what enlightenment means. Respond to this one question. "What kind of revolution was the Enlightenment?" Teacher repeats the question. Students begin writing. The teacher tells them to just write their opinion because they do not have time to use text-dependent evidence to answer the question.
- During the interview and stated in the Interview Protocol for a Pre-Observation (Planning) Conference document, the teacher shares how she will ensure the learning of all students. She explains her process for placing students in homogeneous pair groupings for text readings and annotations. The analyses of the texts are scaffold for students needing more supports, based on their benchmark assessment scores and her observations. The scaffolding includes guides and examples of model responses for annotations, text-dependent question stems, and sample text-dependent responses. For today's lesson, she places students in mixed-ability pairs for crafting text-dependent responses. She selected pairs by reviewing individual student strengths, and pairing those who were strong in some of the skills needed for this activity with those students who may need further development. The teacher anticipates that students may struggle with the conclusion that "the Age of Enlightenment was a revolution of thought, rather than action." The Enlightenment was an intellectual movement, which may be difficult for some students to conclude on their own. In an effort to bridge the gap, students will be focusing on questions provided at the beginning of the class that relate to the concept of "Revolution."
- Three samples of partner work are provided. In the three samples of work, students cite text-dependent evidence in answering the questions.

Record of Evidence

Cluster 5:   Successful Learning by All Students

Interpretation

- The teacher does not extend the students' learning by sharing examples of why she considered their text-dependent questions good.

- The teacher asks students to respond in groups and then again out loud in front of the other students.

- Students' responses on the iPads and verbally presented indicate most understand the concept of revolution and enlightenment.

- Sometimes the teacher offers specific feedback; other times her response is "good, good, very good."

- The teacher's commentary video and planning document reflect the teacher's efforts to ensure the learning of all students. She selected the appropriate text based on the students' reading levels, used information from benchmark testing and her own observations to group students, and used the Gradual Release Model.

- Based on the three student samples of work provided, it appears the students were able to successfully complete the assignment of responding to text-dependent questions created by their peers.

Record of Evidence

Cluster 6:   Professionalism

Guiding Questions

- *To what extent does the teacher engage with the professional community (within the school and beyond) and demonstrate a commitment to ongoing professional learning?*

- *Does the teacher collaborate productively with colleagues and contribute to the life of the school?*

- *Does the teacher engage in professional learning and take a leadership role in the school to promote the welfare of students?*

Evidence

No evidence of Cluster 6 is present in this Instructional Set.

Appendix A: The FFT Clusters
Study Guide Series Team

Ron Anderson, EdD; OH. Danielson Group Consultant.

Dauna Easley, MEd; OH. University of Cincinnati supervisor for student teachers.

Nancy Flickinger, MEd; OH. National Board Certified (AYA/ELA), Teaching Professions Academy Instructor.

Linda Goodwin, MEd; AR. Arkansas LEADS/TESS Support Consultant, Arkansas School Improvement Specialist, Arkansas Quest Leadership Mentor for Administrators, Danielson Group Consultant.

Bobbie Grice, MEd; OH. Resident Educator Coordinator.

Shirley Hall, MEd; NJ. President, GreenLight for Learning, LLC; Former School and District Administrator, Danielson Group Member.

Donna Hanby, PhD; OH. Educational Consultant (Assessment & Accreditation): Educator Preparation Programs.

Kathleen Hanson, MEd; ID. Hanson Educational Consulting, Danielson Group Consultant.

MaryLou McGirr, MEd; SD. Learning Specialist, Technology & Innovation in Education; Trainer for Cognitive Coaching; Danielson Group Consultant.

Joanie Peterson, MEd; OR. Human Resources/ Professional Development Administrator; Danielson Group Consultant.

Sue Presler, MEd; NE. Training Associate, Thinking Collaborative. Trainer for Cognitive Coaching, Adaptive Schools, and Habits of Mind, Danielson Group Member.

Carol Rauch, EdD; OH. University of Cincinnati supervisor for student teachers and Associate Director of Professional Development; Danielson Group Consultant.

Cynthia M. Tocci, PhD; VA. Educational Observations, LLC, Danielson Group Director of Instructional Design.

Appendix B:
List of Study Guide Sets

Set No.	Subject	Grade
1	ELA	8
	Math	3
	Social Studies	11
2	Tech	9
	ELA	8
	Math	4
3	Math	9-10
	ELA	2
	Social Studies	7
4	ELA	12
	Math	2
	Social Studies	9
5	Science & Tech	4
	Math	11
	ELA	7
6	Math	10
	ELA	5
	Math	K
7	Math	6
	ELA	9
	Math	1
8	ELA	K
	ELA	4
	Math	9

Vision

Each educator and student experiences a safe and inclusive learning environment that promotes joyful inquiry, efficacy, intellectual rigor, and reflection grounded in the Framework for Teaching.

Mission

To advance the principles of the Framework for Teaching by partnering with educators and policy leaders at all levels to strengthen professional practices and promote education policies that elevate teacher development and leadership in service of student learning.

Made in the USA
San Bernardino, CA
24 June 2019